The Beginner's Guide to
Computers and the Internet

by Susan Holden
and Matthew Francis

SUMMERSDALE

Summersdale Publishers Ltd
46 West Street
Chichester
West Sussex
PO19 1RP
UK

www.summersdale.com

Printed and bound in Great Britain

ISBN 1 84024 061 X

Warning and Disclaimer

Every effort has been made to make this book as accurate as possible. The authors and publishers shall have neither responsibility nor liability to any person or entity with respect to any loss or damage arising from information contained in this book.

While every effort has been made to trace copyright holders, Summersdale Publishers apologise in advance for any unintentional omission or neglect and will be pleased to insert appropriate acknowledgement to companies or individuals in any subsequent edition of this publication.

Acknowledgements

AOL screenshots copyright © 2001 America Online, Inc. Used with permission.

With thanks to Valerie Enes at the Porter Novelli Convergence Group for permission to cite QUALCOMM Eudora.

Microsoft screenshots copyright © the Microsoft Corporation, reprinted by permission. MSN, Microsoft, MS DOS, Windows and Internet Explorer are registered trademarks and the Office Assistant is a character logo of the Microsoft Corporation.

Netscape screenshots copyright © the Netscape Communications Corporation. Netscape and the Netscape N and Ship's Wheel logos are registered trademarks of Netscape Communications Corporation in the US and other countries.

Yahoo screenshots copyright © Yahoo! Inc. Yahoo!, the Yahoo! Logo and other Yahoo! Logos and product and service names are trademarks of Yahoo! Inc.

AltaVista screenshots © AltaVista. AltaVista ® is a registered trademark and The Search Company and the AltaVista logo are trademarks of AltaVista company.

Lycos screenshots copyright © 2001 Lycos, Inc. Lycos ® is a registered trademark of Carnegie Mellon University. All rights reserved.

With thanks to Janet and Dick Benton for their kind permission to reprint the British Manchester Terrier Club home page.

Excite screenshots copyright © 2001 Excite UK Ltd. With thanks to Ben Starkie.

NovaLogic screenshots copyright © 2001 NovaLogic.

Gamesdomain screenshots copyright © British Telecommunications plc. Gamesdomain.co.uk is the trading name of Games Domain, a division of BTopenworld which is a division of British Telecommunications plc.

Bonus.com screenshots copyright © Bonus.com Inc, a Delaware corporation and are used with permission.

All images used are the property of and copyright of the companies concerned. Use of the material belonging to the above mentioned companies is not meant to convey any endorsement of this book.

Authors' Acknowledgements

The authors are greatly indebted to friends, family and neighbours for their help and tolerance. We would especially like to record our appreciation to Irene Richardson, Peter Fullbrook and David Camp for their practical assistance and advice. Our thanks to those who were kind enough to read and trial early material which formed the basis for some sections of this book, in particular Bernard Amps, Jim Penn, Stan Kirby and Marlene Booker. Our gratitude to Peggy, Pauline, John, Stan and Irene for their interest and encouragement ('Hello! How's the book going?').

Finally, thank you to our editor Rachael Osborne for her good humour, patience and encouragement.

*To our parents Margaret and George,
and Sydney and Margaret, with love.*

Introduction

This book makes the assumption that the reader has no prior knowledge of computing. It uses everyday language and tries to describe procedures and terms in the simplest way possible. The emphasis is on action and success without wasting time in long technical explanations or terms. Each section is divided up into separate sections that contain essential information about each topic. These are followed by a series of actions designed to lead to successful use of computer applications. These easy steps introduce and develop some of the most useful areas of the computer, including using the Internet and e-mail. It also covers the basic word processing elements common to Office 97, Office 2000 and Works 2000. We have included a Jargon Buster at the back of the book to explain any unfamiliar terms.

People who are busy, with little patience, or who simply cannot face anything more technical than a pencil sharpener, will find that this book helps them key into one of the world's most widely-used pieces of technology.

Chapter One:
How to Get Started

Chapter Two:
How To Use Word

Contents

Chapter Three:
How To Use Microsoft Help

Chapter Four:
How to Play Computer Games

Chapter Five:
How to Use Disks

Chapter Six:
How to Stay in Control of Your PC

Contents

Chapter Seven:
How to Create and Manage Files

Chapter Eight:
How to Get Connected to the Internet

Chapter Nine:
How to Use the World Wide Web

Chapter Ten:
How to Use E-mail

Chapter Eleven:
How to Keep Your Computer Healthy

Chapter One:
How to Get Started

Section 1:
Switching On

Essential Information

Check that all the leads of your set-up are connected. Many new computers have cables and terminals which are colour-coded to make them easy to use.

If you are uncertain about the connections, get someone experienced or a computer engineer to check them out for you. It might be a good idea to ask them to colour-code the connections for future reference.

Action 1

Locate the switches on the **monitor** (like the switch on a television, under the screen) and the **systems unit** (the rectangular box with slots for disks) and press each one to switch on. Wait while the computer starts or 'boots up'.

As the computer boots up, the monitor will show a black screen with systems details showing in white text. Allow the computer to continue this process without interference.

Eventually the monitor will display the **Microsoft Windows** symbol. This will then give way to what is called the **desktop**.

Section 2:
The Desktop

Essential Information

The **desktop** (Fig. 1) is a background that houses small pictures called **icons**.

The **taskbar** is a grey strip that is usually positioned across the bottom of the screen. The **Start** button sits on one end of the taskbar and the computer clock at the other.

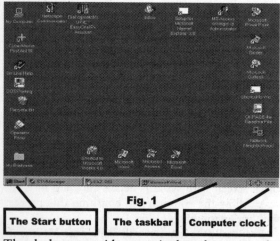

Fig. 1

| The Start button | The taskbar | Computer clock |

The desktop provides a springboard to enter the various programs on your computer.

Section 3:
Icons

The **icons** are designed to give you a clue about the program that they are meant to represent. For example, a picture of a waste bin represents the Recycle Bin which is where you can send any unwanted items or documents.

Icons are shortcuts that have been created to lead straight into a program, activity or even a document that you have created. Each different picture represents a unique program or item on your computer. Later you will discover how to create these shortcuts yourself.

Section 4:
The Mouse

Essential Information
The mouse will have two (sometimes three) buttons on the top and a ball set in the underside.

Uses of the mouse:
1. Moves a pointer on the screen.
2. By moving the pointer and clicking on the left button, various functions can be performed on the screen.

3. By using the right mouse button in conjunction with the pointer, more complicated functions can be performed.

Action 1
Place the palm of your writing hand lightly over the body of the mouse. Your fingers should be resting over the buttons. Move the mouse forward and backward on the mouse mat so that the ball on the underside is moved.

Action 2
Once again, move the mouse and notice how the pointer moves across the desktop on the computer screen. Notice that the pointer at this stage is in the shape of an arrow. The arrow on the screen moves in the same direction as the mouse.

Action 3
Move the pointer to the four sides of the screen.

Top Tip
Don't worry if it takes a little time to become co-ordinated – most adults do.
Just practise and be patient with yourself.

Section 5:
Clicking

Essential Information

The left mouse button is almost always used for clicking. There are two types of clicking: single and double.

Action 1

Place the forefinger of your writing hand over the left mouse button and press once. This is a single click. Now press twice in rapid succession. This is called a double-click.

Practise double-clicking, as it does take some people a considerable time to get the hang of it. Do not be concerned if you find this difficult as the computer can be adjusted to your speed (Section 9).

Top Tip

There is an alternative if you have problems with double-clicking. When instructions call for a double-click, use a single click and then press the Return button (Section 7).

Action 2

The click and drag technique is used to move objects or text.

Move the pointer onto the **My Computer** icon. Click once and hold your finger down. Do not release the left-hand button. Whilst the button remains depressed, move the pointer across the screen, and if you are doing it correctly you will also move the icon. Release the button and the icon will stay in the new position.

Now try moving the other icons across the screen. Release them and then move them back again.

Top Tip
Be neat – leave your desktop looking tidy!

Section 6:
Pointers

The pointer will change shape according to the task that it is performing. Figure 2 shows the shapes that you will encounter in this section of the book. The appearance of the egg timer means that you need to wait for a task to be completed.

Fig. 2

normal arrow pointer   **working**   **busy**

When the computer has finished performing a task the pointer will return to the normal arrow shape.

Section 7:
Introducing the Keyboard

Essential Information
Computer keyboards can vary greatly but they do all contain the same functions – it's just a case of locating them. The main groups of keys are shown in Figure 3.

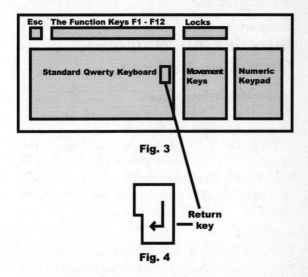

Fig. 3

Fig. 4

Action 1

Locate the Return key. This can be various shapes but it will probably have an arrow on it like the one in Figure 4. Some keyboards have the words 'Return' or 'Enter' written on the key.

This key has a number of uses but in this section it will be used to help open various programs on the computer. For the moment, just be aware of the name and location of this important key. You will meet other uses for it later on.

Section 8:
Introducing Windows, Menus and Boxes

Essential Information

A window shows what is contained within the program represented by an icon.

For example, on the desktop is the Recycle Bin. Imagine that it is an ordinary waste bin where you put your rubbish. If you open the Recycle Bin by double-clicking on the icon, a window appears displaying the contents.

Action 1

Move the pointer onto the Recycle Bin icon and click once. The icon changes colour. Press Return on your keyboard. A window opens as in Figure 5a.

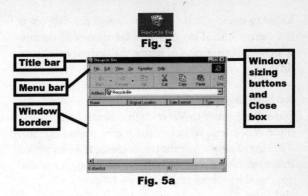

Fig. 5

Fig. 5a

At the moment the Recycle Bin is empty, hence the blank window.

Action 2

Look at the following features of the window in Figure 5a. All windows have them.

1. The edges are defined by the **window border**.
2. Along the top of the window is a **title bar**. This changes colour when selected and is also used for moving the window.
3. In the top right-hand corner are the **sizing buttons**. For more on these, see page 99.
4. Next to the sizing buttons is the **Close box** (denoted by a cross). By clicking on the cross the window will be closed.

21

5. Along the top of the window below the title bar is the **menu bar**. This contains the names of menus, which are your means of telling the computer what to do.

Action 3

Move the pointer to **View** on the menu bar, and click once. A box appears below the View option (Fig. 5b). This list of words is a **menu**. A menu is a box with a list of words which are options that you can use to control the computer. Menus are found on windows and some boxes.

To remove the menu, move the pointer off the menu and onto the window, click once and the menu disappears.

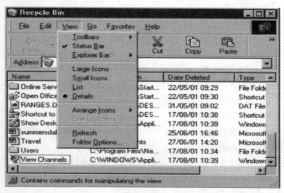

Fig. 5b

Action 4

Boxes also enable you to tell the computer what to do. The following are some of the more common ones. They will be covered in more detail later.

Text boxes.
These are boxes into which you can type (see page 118).

Drop-down list boxes.
Further items are displayed by clicking on a downward pointing arrow (see page 54).

Command buttons.
These allow you to decide a course of action, e.g., to Save, Cancel or Display (see page 25).

Radio buttons.
These are circles with black dots in the centre. By clicking on a circle you cause a black dot to either appear or disappear. This is a method used for selecting options (see page 25).

Check boxes.
These are another way of making a selection. By clicking on a check box you cause a tick to either appear or disappear (see page 199).

Section 9:
Customising your Clicking Speed

Essential Information

The computer has got to be able to recognise the difference between a single click and a double-click. If your double-click is too slow it will appear to the computer as two single clicks.

We all click at different speeds. In response to this, your Microsoft application has been designed to allow you to customise the computer to a clicking speed that is comfortable for you. To do this you need to go to the Mouse Properties window.

Action 1

Move the pointer onto the **Start** button, click once, and the Start menu appears. Move the pointer up to **Settings**, then across to the **Control Panel** and click once. This path is shown in Figure 6.

Fig. 6
The path to the Control Panel

If you have followed the correct path, the Control Panel window will open (Fig. 7).

24

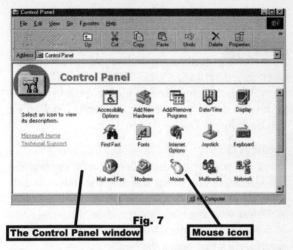

Fig. 7

| The Control Panel window | Mouse icon |

Click once on the mouse icon. Press Return on your keyboard and you will open Mouse Properties (Fig. 8).

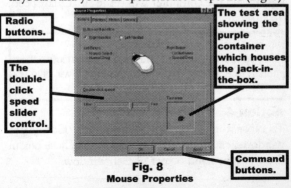

Radio buttons.

The test area showing the purple container which houses the jack-in-the-box.

The double-click speed slider control.

Command buttons.

Fig. 8
Mouse Properties

Action 2

To test your clicking speed, move the pointer onto the test area. Try double-clicking on the purple box. If your clicking speed corresponds to the current double-click speed setting, a jack-in-the-box will appear. Double-click again to return him to the box.

If you cannot open the box, the double-click speed can be reduced. Follow Action 3.

Action 3

Place the pointer on the slider control, depress the left button, hold it down and drag the slider towards Slow (i.e. click and drag).

Retest your double-click speed on the purple box and adjust the slider control until you achieve a double-click that opens the box.

Once you are happy with the adjustment, click on **Apply** and the computer will set itself at that speed. To close the window, click once on OK.

Top Tip

If you are left-handed and wish to reconfigure the mouse to a left-handed option, page 197 will give you directions.

Action 4

To close the Control Panel and My Computer windows, click once on the cross in the Close box in the top right-hand corner of each window.

Section 10:
Opening a Program

Essential Information

There are two ways to open a program:

1. Through an icon on the desktop. This can be achieved by a single click on the icon and then pressing Return or just double-clicking on the icon.
2. By going to the Start button and navigating the Start menu (follow Actions 1 – 2).

Action 1

Move the pointer onto the Start button and click once. A menu appears (Fig. 9).

**Note the small arrow
by some items in the
menu. This is an
indication of another
menu.**

Fig. 9

27

Action 2

Move the pointer up the menu to **Programs**. Another menu appears showing the programs listed on your computer (see Fig. 10). Move the pointer onto one of the programs and click once. The program will open onto the screen.

Close the program by clicking on the Close box.

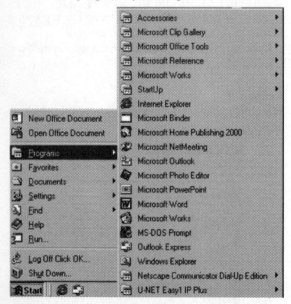

Fig. 10
The path to Programs.

Section 11:
Introducing Office and Works Programs

Essential Information

Microsoft Office 97 and 2000 have three distinct sections to them that will enable you to produce documents, create spreadsheets and compile databases. Each section has a different name and icon.

Microsoft Word for producing documents

Microsoft Excel for producing spreadsheets

Microsoft Access for producing databases

Double-clicking on the appropriate icon on the desktop will take you straight into a program.

Another route is through Programs on the Start menu (Fig. 10).

Works 2000

Microsoft Works 2000 is a package that allows you to create documents, spreadsheets, databases and many other things besides.

To access them you need to open the **Works Task Launcher** from the icon on the desktop,

or through **Programs** on the **Start** menu (Fig. 10).

This book will be looking at the word processing part of Office and Works but not at spreadsheets and databases. However, many of the features of word processing are common to the other programs and can be applied to them. *Chapter Two: How to Use Word* will show you how to operate within Office and Works.

Section 12:
Mouse Control and Solitaire

Essential Information
To practise mouse control, clicking, and clicking and dragging, the game of Solitaire is very useful. Solitaire is also known as Patience.

Action 1
Go to Start and click once, then click on Programs, Accessories, Games and Solitaire. This path is shown in Figure 11.

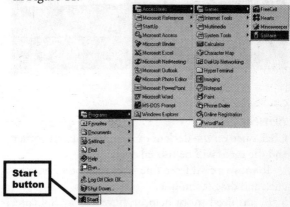

Fig. 11
Path to Games and Solitaire

31

When you reach Solitaire, click once and Solitaire opens (Fig. 12).

> **These four empty spaces are to house the four aces when they appear. Try clicking and dragging them into the spaces or double-clicking on the ace to move it.**

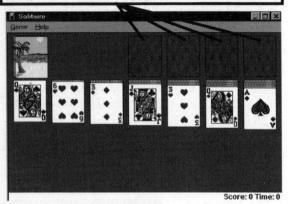

Fig. 12
Solitaire

Action 2

Click once on the deck of cards in the top left corner and the cards will be turned over.

To move a card from one place to another, use the click and drag technique.

If you need more help on how to play Solitaire, click on the **Help** button at the top. The Help drop-down menu opens (Fig. 13).

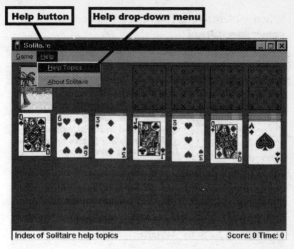

Fig. 13

Click once on **Help Topics**. Help Topics opens as in Figure 14. Click once on **How to Play Solitaire** so that it becomes highlighted in blue. Then click on the **Display** button.

Fig. 14
Help Topics: Solitaire Help

Solitaire Help opens (Fig. 15).

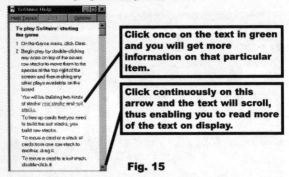

Fig. 15

To remove Display, click on the Close box. You will be returned back to Solitaire.

Action 3
When you have finished playing the game, close it down by clicking on the Close box.

Top Tip
You might be keen to conquer your computer and consequently regard playing Solitaire as a waste of time. It really isn't. It's a valuable lesson in mouse control and other techniques, so do have a go!

Section 13:
Shutting Down

Essential Information

There is a set procedure to follow to shut down your computer.

Before you shut down, always close any windows still open by clicking once on the Close box. You should then be looking at the desktop.

Action 1

Click once on Start with the pointer.

Highlight **Shut Down**.

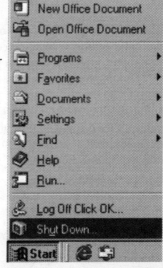

Fig. 16

35

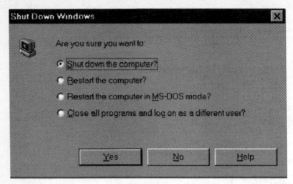

Fig. 17

The **Shut Down Windows** box appears. Check that the radio button is highlighted by 'Shut down the computer?' (Fig. 17). Click on 'Yes'.

The computer will close down its program and then one of two things will happen: your computer will automatically switch itself off *or* the following message will appear: 'It is safe to turn off your computer.'

At this point you will need to switch off the systems unit and monitor manually.

Chapter Two:
How to Use Word

Section 1:
What is Word Processing?

Essential Information

Microsoft Word has a wide range of tools that, among other things, manipulate text. These tools are very easy to use and it's just a case of getting used to them.

The word processing program contains characters, numbers, styles and designs which, using the tools and your skill plus the wizardry of the computer, can create professional documents. There are many functions that the Word program will perform automatically to format your text correctly, such as when you type the **st** of 1st or the **th** of 6th the computer will cause the double letters to automatically jump to the correct position by the number (make sure that you press the space bar once after typing the double letters, otherwise this function will not operate).

Any Problems?

If you have any difficulties whilst using Word, try using the Help button, the Office Assistant or What's This? For more information about these facilities, read *Chapter Three: How to Use Microsoft Help.*

Section 2:
Opening the Word Processing Program

Essential Information

Word processing is present on Office 97, Office 2000 and Works 2000. Works is opened in a different way to Office so follow Action 2.

Action 1 (Office 97 and Office 2000)

Look for a shortcut icon on the desktop (Fig. 1). Double-click on the icon and it will take you straight into the word processing program.

Fig. 1

Alternatively, click on the **Start** button and from the Start menu select **Programs**. On the second menu that appears you will find **Microsoft Word** listed. Move the pointer across onto this second menu and allow it to rest on Microsoft Word and a double-click will lead you into the word processing program.

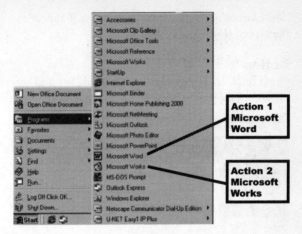

Fig. 2

Action 2 (Microsoft Works 2000)

To open the word processing part of Works you need
to activate the Works Task Launcher, which opens the
Microsoft Works Suite. To do this, follow the pathway to Programs, and then double-click
on **Microsoft Works** (Fig. 2), or alternatively look for a shortcut icon on the
desktop and double-click (Fig. 3).

Fig. 3

The Microsoft Works Suite Window will appear on the screen (Fig. 4).

Action 3

Click once on **Programs** on the black bar and the different programs will be listed on the left.

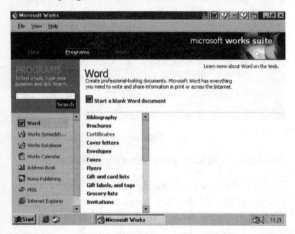

Fig. 4

Look at the section below the black bar and you will see the phrase 'Start a blank Word document'. Move the pointer onto this phrase and the arrow will turn into a hand. Double-click and you will be taken straight into the word processing program.

Section 3:
The Word Window

Essential Information
The basic functions of word processing in Office 97, Office 2000 and Works 2000 are essentially the same. Any important differences will be noted in the appropriate place.

Action 1
Once you have opened your word processing program, the Microsoft Word window will appear on the screen. Identify the following features:

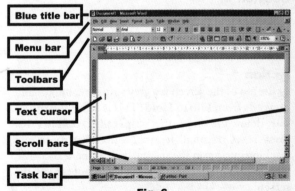

Fig. 6
Word window on Office 2000 and Works 2000

41

Fig. 6a
The Word window on Office 97

On Office 97, each individual page has its own title bar, so you will see two blue title bars: one for Microsoft Word and one for the document that is currently being viewed.

Section 4:
Features of the Word Window

Action 1

At the top of the screen is a grey strip containing a line of words from **File** to **Help**. This is called the **menu bar**. Below this are further strips called **toolbars** that carry rows of small icons. Notice that there is a blinking cursor on the screen. This is the text cursor, which indicates where the text will appear on the screen.

Action 2

Move the pointer over the white page and notice when it changes from an arrow into an **I**. This shape is called an I-beam. Move it onto the toolbars at the top of the page and it will return to an arrow.

Action 3

Look at Figure 7 and identify the scroll bar. This is a device that enables you to see more of the page on the screen. The screen can only show a small portion of a page at any one time. Try clicking on the upward or downward pointing arrow and you will see that the page can be scrolled vertically to reveal more of the document. It can also be scrolled horizontally.

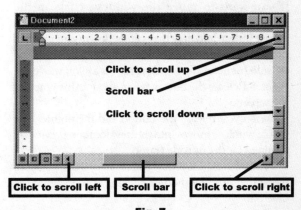

Fig. 7

A vertical scroll bar is always on the right-hand side of the page. The horizontal scroll bar is always at the bottom of the page.

Action 4

On Office 97 (Fig. 6a), notice that the name of the document ('Document 2') is on the blue title bar at the top of the page. On Office 2000 and Works 2000 (Fig. 6) the name of the document ('Document 1') is on the Microsoft blue bar.

Every time you open a document its name will be present on the title bar.

Action 5

If you want to move the window, click on the Microsoft Word blue title bar, hold down the left mouse button and drag the pointer downward towards the bottom of the screen. You will notice that only the outside frame of the window moves as you move the pointer. Release the button when about halfway across the screen.

When you release the button and the pointer, the whole window moves into the new location previously outlined by the outside frame.

Now move the window back to its original position, using the same method of clicking and dragging the blue bar.

In Office 97 the individual pages can also be moved in this way, by clicking and dragging on the blue title bar.

Section 5:
Opening a New Document

Essential Information
Upon opening up the Microsoft Word program, a new clean page is displayed on the screen. Once this page has been utilised however, you will need to know how to open another new document. For Office 97 and Office 2000 read Actions 1 – 4. For Works 2000 read Actions 5 – 7.

Action 1 (Office 97 and Office 2000)
Move the pointer to the top of the screen and onto the menu bar. Notice that the I-beam has changed to an arrow. Place the arrow on the word **File** (extreme left-hand corner), and click once. A new drop-down menu will appear (Fig. 8).

Action 2
Move the pointer down the menu and the items will be highlighted in blue. Move the pointer onto the word **New** and click once with the left mouse button.

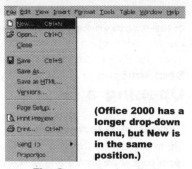

(Office 2000 has a longer drop-down menu, but New is in the same position.)

Fig. 8
Office 97

Action 3

A box opens, with **Blank Document** highlighted in blue (Fig. 9).

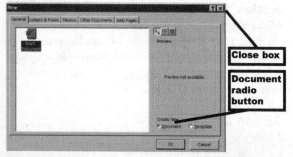

Close box

Document radio button

Fig. 9
Office 97

(Office 2000 looks the same but with more icons)

46

Make sure that the radio button by **Document**, in the bottom right-hand corner, is activated. It should contain a black dot. If it doesn't, click in the white circle once. Click **OK** in the bottom right corner and a new blank page opens, ready for you to begin work.

Action 4
To close this page, click once on the cross in the Close box.

Action 5 (Works 2000)
Move the pointer to the top of the screen and onto the menu bar. Notice that the I-beam has changed to an arrow. Place the arrow onto the word **File** (extreme left-hand corner), and click once. A new drop-down menu will appear (Fig. 10).

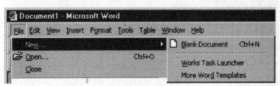

Fig. 10
Works 2000

Action 6
Move the pointer onto the word **New** and a further menu appears. Click once on **Blank Document** and a new page opens immediately.

Action 7
To close the page, click once on the cross in the Close box.

Section 6:
Moving Around the Page Using the Keyboard

Essential Information

The keyboard, as well as the mouse, allows you to interact with the computer and move text and the cursor around the page. If you have previously used a typewriter then you will be familiar with the layout of the computer keyboard, which adheres to the traditional 'Qwerty' format. Besides having normal keyboard functions, the computer keyboard can also be used to give additional commands to the word processing program.

The space bar is in the centre of the bottom row of the keyboard and allows you to put a space between text. If you keep pressing the space bar, the blinking text cursor will move across the page. It can also be used to move text about the page and into the correct place.

Top Tip

If you cannot initially see the blinking text cursor, then move the mouse pointer onto the page, click once and it should appear.

Identify the **Return** key on your keyboard (Fig. 11).

Fig. 11

It is sometimes called the Enter key. In word processing it allows you to move the text cursor down the page and to put line spaces between sentences.

Section 7:
Creating Text, Deleting and the I-Beam

Essential Information

Once the blinking text cursor is visible on the screen you can begin to type.

Do not worry about capitals at this point. Remind yourself where Return is located on your keyboard and also find the Delete key before you begin to type. Remember, when the pointer moves onto the white area of the page it appears as an I-beam.

Action 1

Make sure you are looking at a blank page. Type your

name and then press Return. Notice that the text cursor has moved down a line. Type the rest of your address, remembering to press Return at the end of each line.

As soon as the text cursor reaches the end of a line it will automatically move down. This is called the **Wraparound** feature and it allows you to keep on typing without bothering to press the Return key in order to start a new line.

Action 2

Move the pointer to the centre of one of the words that you have just typed, and click once with the left mouse button. Notice that the I-beam has moved the blinking text cursor to the place where you have just clicked. This is an important action in allowing you to alter and delete text.

Action 3

Delete

Fig. 12

The **Delete** key (Fig. 12) removes text from the **right** of the text cursor.

Move the mouse pointer to the centre of a word

that you have typed and click once. Press the Delete key once and notice that a letter from the right of the text cursor has been deleted. If you keep your finger depressed on the Delete key, the text is deleted rapidly. Repeat this procedure to delete all the text that you have just typed.

The **Backspace** key (Fig. 13) removes letters to the **left** of the cursor.

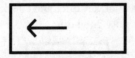

Fig. 13

Section 8:
Capitals, 'Caps Lock' and the Shift Key

Essential Information
To type capitals you can use the **Capitals Lock** key or the **Shift** key.

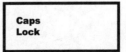

Fig. 14

Press the Capitals Lock key (Fig. 14) once and a light comes on at the top right of your keyboard, showing that the key is activated. Press Caps Lock once again and the light will go out.

Action 1

If you wish all the text to be in capitals, then press the Caps Lock key and make sure that the Caps Lock light has come on. Type the text. To return to lower case, press the Caps Lock key once and check that the Caps Lock light has now gone out.

Fig. 15

Action 2

You will find a **Shift** key (Fig. 15) on both sides of the keyboard.

To type a capital using the Shift key, press the Shift key and hold it down whilst you type the letter. When you release the Shift key you are returned to lower case.

Section 9:
The Formatting Toolbar and Font Boxes

Essential Information

Across the top of the screen are a series of grey strips called toolbars. There are a variety of different toolbars, all with different names, which you can customise to appear on the screen. One toolbar allows you to format the text on the screen and is therefore called the Formatting toolbar.

Action 1

Look at Figure 16 of the Formatting toolbar.

Fig. 16

The various functions on this toolbar allow you to alter the style of your document.

Action 2

Identify the two font boxes on the picture of the Formatting toolbar (Fig. 17).

Font style
(style of text)
Font size
(size of text)

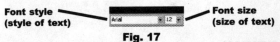

Fig. 17

Times New Roman will normally appear as the font style because it is the **default** style set by the computer.

JARGON BUSTER
Default

Default means a preselected setting that the
computer will open as its first choice.

Action 3

To choose a different font, click on the black triangle (down arrow) to the right of the font box. A drop-down list appears showing all the font styles (Fig. 18).

Clicking on the down arrow (black triangle) produces a drop-down list of styles. The drop-down list also has a scroll bar; clicking on the down arrow above or below the scroll bar allows you to move up and down the list of font styles.

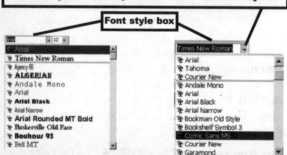

Fig. 18

Office 2000   Office 97 and Works 2000

Action 4

Move the pointer up and down the list and each font will be highlighted in turn.

Select a font style that appeals to you and click once. The new style will have replaced Times New Roman as the font style.

Action 5

The computer usually sets the default font size at 10. However, font size 12 is one of the most frequently used sizes for documents.

Click on the down arrow to the right of the font size box. A drop-down list appears showing the font sizes.

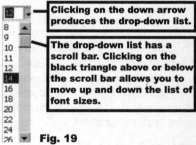

Clicking on the down arrow produces the drop-down list.

The drop-down list has a scroll bar. Clicking on the black triangle above or below the scroll bar allows you to move up and down the list of font sizes.

Fig. 19

As the pointer is moved up and down the list, each font size is highlighted in turn. Select a different size font and click once with the left-hand mouse button to change the font size to your personal choice.

Section 10:
Highlighting Text

Essential Information
Being able to highlight text is very important in producing documents. The trick is in moving the pointer slowly and staying off the margin.

Action 1
Type a single line of text. Place the I-beam on the same line as the text and carefully move the pointer to the left until it changes from an I-beam into an arrow.

Position the pointer to left of the text, so that the arrow points towards the words.

 John Smith

If the arrow is pointing *away* from your name you have probably moved off the page and onto the margin. If so, move the pointer back onto your name so that it once again becomes an I-beam and try again, this time more slowly and staying on the white page and on the same line as your name.

Action 2
Once you have the arrow pointing towards the text, click once on the left mouse button and the words will be highlighted.

e.g. John Smith

Action 3

To highlight part of your name, place the pointer at the beginning of the part you wish to highlight and, keeping the left mouse button depressed, move the cursor slowly over the letters.

Action 4

Click once onto a white part of the screen and the highlight disappears.

Top Tip

It's a good idea to practise the technique of highlighting until you get the hang of it.

It is also possible to highlight a whole document in order to make changes that apply to all of the text.

Action 5

Move the I-beam to the left of the text, until the I-beam changes to an arrow, pointing towards the text. Click once on the left-hand button, hold it down and drag the arrow downwards until all the text is highlighted. Release the left mouse button.

Action 6

While the text is highlighted you can make any changes that you wish, such as italicising or deleting text.

Action 7

Click anywhere on the page and the black highlight will disappear.

Section 11:
Bold, Italic and Underline Buttons

Essential Information

The Formatting toolbar also allows you to change the appearance of text in more ways than just altering size and style. Also found on the formatting toolbar are the **bold**, *italic* and underlining functions. These text formatting buttons allow you to make even more changes to your document.

Action 1

Identify these buttons on the formatting toolbar:

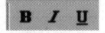

BUTTONS

B is used to em**bold**en the text.

I is used to make the text *italic*.

<u>U</u> is used to underline.

Action 2

Type a piece of text that it is at least four lines long, for example:

Special Offer at your Local Store

To all our customers:
Sale ends on Saturday
Fantastic bargains still available
Don't miss out!

John Smith
(Sales Director)

Top Tip

To type brackets, press and hold down the
Shift key at the same time as typing the bracket.

Shift key

The Shift key is present on the left and right of the
keyboard and carries a large upward pointing arrow.

Action 3

Highlight the title of the document 'Special Offers at Your Local Store'.

Click once on the **Bold** button. Click once on the white page and the highlight disappears, showing the text emphasised in bold. Notice that the Bold button is now depressed and appears a lighter grey. This shows that you have activated the Bold function.

Action 4

Highlight the rest of the text. Click once on *Italic*. Click on the white page to remove the highlight and the whole of the text is now shown in italics.

Action 5

Highlight the title and click on the <u>Underline</u> button. Now click on the white page to remove the highlight and you can see that the title is now underlined.

Action 6

To remove Bold, Italic or Underline, highlight the section of text to be changed and notice that the formatting text button presently in use (i.e. **bold**, *italic* or <u>underlined</u>) will be depressed, and show as a light grey colour.

Click once on whichever button you wish to remove. Notice that the button is no longer depressed and is now the same colour grey as the rest of the bar. The button has been de-activated.

Click on the white page to remove the highlight.

Section 12:
Changing the Colour of Text

Essential Information
The Formatting toolbar also allows you to change the colour of the text, thus enabling you to produce eye-catching documents. Of course, these will only be apparent on paper if you have a colour printer.

Action 1

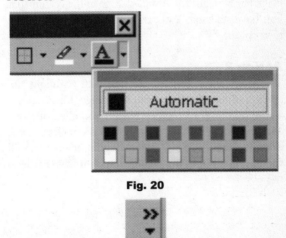

Fig. 20

Fig. 20a

Identify a button with a large letter A on the extreme right of the formatting toolbar (Fig. 20) (If you are using Office 2000 or Works 2000 you may need to click on the toolbar extension to see the font colour button, Fig. 20a). This is the font colour button. Beneath the A is a black bar. This indicates the current colour being used for the text. Notice the downward pointing arrow to the right of the A. Click once on the arrow and a drop-down colour chart is displayed. Click once on whichever colour you wish to use. The black bar beneath the A will change to the colour that you have selected. You can now begin typing in the new colour.

Action 2

To change the colour of existing text, highlight the section of text that you wish to change. Click on the arrow by the Font Colour button and click on your chosen colour from the drop-down colour chart. Click once on the page to remove the highlight and you will then be able to see the change that you have made to the text.

Section 13:
Alignment and Justify

Essential Information

Next to the formatting text buttons are the **Alignment** and **Justify** buttons, which allow you to decide on the positioning of your text on the page.

Align Left will arrange your text to the left of the page, leaving a ragged edge on the right.

Align Right will arrange the text to the right of the page.

Align Center (this is the American spelling used by Microsoft) will arrange the text down the centre of the page.

Justify stretches the text evenly across the page.

Action 1

Identify the four alignment buttons on the formatting toolbar.

Fig. 21

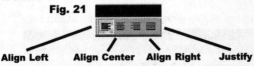

Align Left   Align Center   Align Right   Justify

Action 2

Type a piece of text. Make sure that you have at least four or five lines. Do not press Return. It is highly probable that the text will automatically align left on the page. Look at the Align Left button and notice if it is depressed and a lighter grey than the other buttons. If it is, then the text is already aligned left.

If it is not depressed then highlight the whole of the text and click once on the Align Left button. The text will then be aligned to the left of the page. Click on the page to remove the highlight. Repeat these actions but use the other buttons to align right and to centre the text.

Action 3

Identify the Justify button on the toolbar. It sits next to the alignment buttons.

The Justify button stretches the text across the page to give a neat appearance. To justify text, just highlight it and then click on the Justify button. Click on the page to remove the highlight.

Section 14:
The Menu Bar

At the top of the Word window is the menu bar.

Fig. 22

By clicking onto any one of these words, a drop-down menu will be displayed. The words on each menu represent commands that operate the Word program. Some of the basic commands used in creating word documents will be covered here.

Action 1
Move the pointer onto the menu bar. Observe that the I-beam turns into an arrow. Move the arrow onto each word on the menu bar. Notice that as the arrow rests on each, a grey box around it becomes raised.

Action 2
Place the pointer onto the word **File** and click once. The File drop-down menu is displayed (Fig. 23).

Fig. 23

Action 3
Move the pointer onto other words on the menu bar and 'visit' the other drop-down menus. You will discover more about some of them later. For the moment, all you need to be concerned about is that the menu bar exists!

Section 15:
Undo and Redo

Essential Information

The **Undo** and **Redo** buttons can save you a great deal of time and despair! At some point in time you are bound to make a mistake in your typing or delete text in error. Help is at hand in the shape of the Undo and Redo buttons that will allow you to recall actions and text from the PC memory.

Look at the Standard toolbar and identify the following:

Undo  Redo

Fig. 24

Action 1

Type a few lines on a new page and then highlight the first line of your document. Press the Delete key to remove this line. Now imagine that you have made a mistake and need to retrieve this first line.

Action 2

Move the pointer onto the Undo button. Click once and, as if by magic, the first line of your document reappears.

Action 3

Now imagine that you have reread that first line and it really isn't what you want after all. Move your cursor onto to the Redo button and click once. Your line disappears again because the computer has redone your original action of deleting the first line.

Action 4

It is possible to retrieve more that just one action. Click on the downward pointing arrows by the Undo button. A drop-down list appears showing all your previous actions on this particular document.

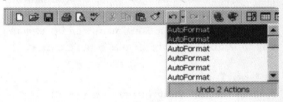

Fig. 25

There is even a scroll bar to enable you to scroll back through the history of your document! You can highlight as many actions as you wish to undo and undo them in one go. The same applies to the Redo button.

Top Tip
Time spent in perfecting the use of these buttons will save you time and anguish later on!

Section 16:
Spelling and Grammar

Essential Information
Identify the **Spelling and Grammar** button (**spell-check**) on the Standard toolbar.

Fig. 26

This button allows the computer to automatically check your work for spelling mistakes. However, it might not recognise personal names and places and may sometimes identify them as being incorrect.

Action 1
Type in the following but do not use all capitals. Include all spelling mistakes.

Mye lif stori begins whenn I was borrn.

As you type, a red line should appear under any word that the computer considers to be incorrect. Any grammatical mistakes are underlined in green.

Action 2

Click on the **spell-check** button. The Spelling and Grammar box appears, highlighting incorrect spellings in red (Fig. 27).

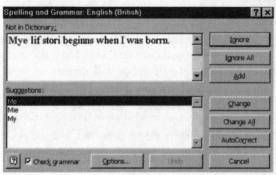

Fig. 27

You now have a choice of two ways to alter the spelling mistake.

1. In the **Suggestions** box will be a selection of alternative spellings. If you wish to use one of these alternatives, click on it, then click on **Change**.

If there is not a suitable alternative listed by the computer, you can correct the spelling yourself by clicking once on the word spelt wrongly and shown in red within the box. The blinking text cursor will then be in position. You are now able to type in the correct spelling. Then click on **Change**.

Action 3

If you do not wish to change the spelling at all (because it is a name or an unusual word) then click on **Ignore**.

The spell-check will continue through the document unless you click on Close. Once the spell-check has finished a small box will appear:

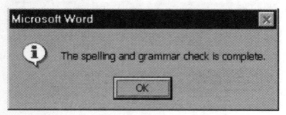

Fig. 28

Click on OK.

Top Tip
After using the Spelling and Grammar function,
read through your document to ensure
that it still makes sense.

Action 4

Type this sentence: My cat wont use the cat flap.

Now click once on the **Spelling and Grammar** button. The Spelling and Grammar window appears and highlights the grammatical error in green.

Action 5

In the suggestion box is an alternative: 'won't'. If you wish to alter the word, then click on **Change** on the right of the window. If you do not wish to alter the word, then click on **Ignore**. If you want to remove the grammar check, click once on the check box and remove the tick.

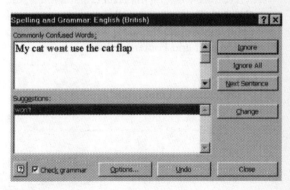

Fig. 29

Section 17:
Headers and Footers

Essential Information

The **Header** is the area of space at the very top of your page and the **Footer** is the area of space at the bottom. Both the Header and Footer give you the opportunity to utilise the whole page.

The title can be placed in the Header section and the Footer section gives space to insert footnotes or page numbers. Anything you wish can be placed in these spaces: logos, graphics, dates, even pictures!

When you are working in Headers and Footers, the text on the main document will fade and so you will not be able to work on the main document until you close the Header and Footer toolbar.

Action 1

Go to **View** on the menu bar and click on **Header and Footer** (Fig. 30).

Fig. 30

Action 2

A new toolbar called **Header and Footer** appears on the screen (Fig. 31).

If you allow the pointer to rest on each symbol, the name of the function will appear on the screen. Identify the various symbols on the toolbar.

Fig. 31

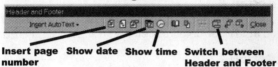

Insert page   **Show date**   **Show time**   **Switch between**
number   **Header and Footer**

Action 3

Click on **Switch between Header and Footer**. This allows you to switch between the top of the page and the bottom. Click on Switch between Header and Footer again and you will be back to where you started.

Click on Close on the Header and Footer toolbar.

Action 4

Open up a document that you have previously saved. If you have not yet saved a document, then create one by typing a few lines. Click on **View**, then click on **Header and Footer**. The new toolbar appears on the screen and also the Header.

The Header will be at the top of the page and will appear as a dotted line box. It will have the word Header in the top left-hand corner of the dotted box.

Action 5

Notice how the writing of your document has faded; this reminds you that while you are working in Headers and Footers you will not be able to write on the main document. The text cursor is already blinking in the Header and is thus ready for you to type. Type in a title for the document.

Action 6

Now go to the Header and Footer toolbar and click once on **Insert Date**. Notice that today's date has been inserted.

Action 7

Click on **Switch between Header and Footer**. You should now be looking at the Footer. If not, click again on **Switch between Header and Footer**.

Action 8

Now click on **Insert Page Number**. Notice that a number has been added to the bottom of the page. Now click on **Insert Time**. Notice that the time has also been added to the Footer.

Action 9

Click on **Close** on the Headers and Footers toolbar. You will now be returned to the main body of your document. Save your document (see p.115).

Action 10

If you want to view the changes that you have made to your document, click on **Print Preview** (**File** then **Print Preview**, p.133) and view it there.

Section 18:
Line Spacing

Essential Information

So far, all your typing has probably been in single line spacing. It is possible, however, to automatically type text in other sizes of spacing.

Action 1

Open Microsoft Word, if not already open, and select a **New** document. Go to **Format** and click once. Click on **Paragraph** (Fig. 32).

Fig. 32

Action 2

A box appears called **Paragraph** (Fig. 33). It has two tabs at the top. Choose **Indents and Spacing**.

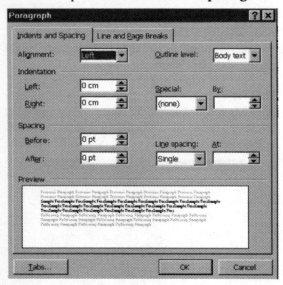

Fig. 33

Action 3

The box contains a number of text boxes. One of them is called **Line spacing**. Within this text box will be written 'Single'. At the side of the box is a triangle (down arrow). Click on it and a drop-down list is displayed (Fig. 34).

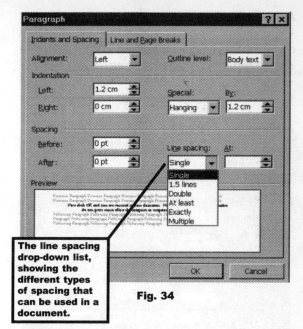

The line spacing drop-down list, showing the different types of spacing that can be used in a document.

Fig. 34

Action 4

Highlight Double and click once. Click **OK** and you are returned to the document. Now type a few lines of text using the Wraparound function; do not press Return.

Because you have already chosen double spacing, your text should automatically be double-spaced.

Action 5

Highlight the document that you have just typed in double spacing. Click on **Format** and then click on **Paragraph**. Find the **Line spacing** box and this time select Single spacing and click on OK. You are returned to your document and the text is now in single spacing.

Action 6

The Paragraph box also allows you to change the alignment of your text.

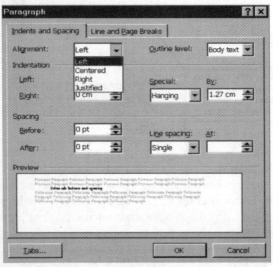

Fig. 35

Look at the top left-hand side of the box and find the title called **Alignment** (Fig. 35). Click on the down arrow and a drop-down list appears. Here you will see the words, Left, Centered, Right and Justified. These perform the same functions as the alignment buttons on the Formatting toolbar. Going through Paragraph is just another way of reaching this function, and if you are changing your line spacing it may well be quicker for you to select the alignment of your document at the same time.

Section 19:
Cursor Keys

Essential Information
Identify the buttons below on the keyboard (Fig. 36). These allow you to move the blinking text cursor to the top or bottom of the page and to the right and left. They will only work when there is text on the page.

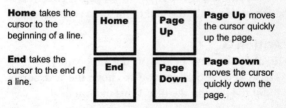

Home takes the cursor to the beginning of a line.

End takes the cursor to the end of a line.

Page Up moves the cursor quickly up the page.

Page Down moves the cursor quickly down the page.

Fig. 36

Action 1

Open up any document that you have saved or type a few lines of text.

Click at the beginning of any line of text. Now press the cursor key **End**.

Notice that the text cursor has travelled to the end of the line.

Now press the cursor key **Home**. The text cursor has travelled to the beginning of the line.

Action 2

At the bottom of the text, click on the very last letter that you have typed. Now press the cursor key **Page Up**. Your text cursor will progress up the page. Keep pressing until the cursor reaches the very first letter on the first line.

Now press the cursor key **Page Down**. The text cursor progresses down the page. As you press, watch the scroll bar on the right of the page. This moves downwards, until the end of the page is reached.

Action 3

Identify the keys below on the keyboard (Fig. 37). These keys also allow you to move the text cursor about the page in the directions indicated.

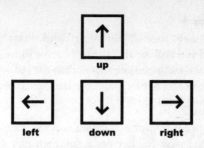

Fig. 37

Action 4

On the page that you have open at the moment, experiment with moving the text cursor around the text, using just the cursor keys.

Section 20:
The Tab Key

Essential Information

Identify the **Tab** key on your keyboard. This key allows you to create paragraphs, columns and matching spaces in a document.

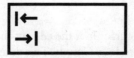

Fig. 38

81

Action 1

Open a new page in Microsoft Word. Press the Tab key and you will see that the text cursor moves across the screen taking bigger spaces than the space bar. To return the text cursor, press the Backspace key.

Action 2

Make sure that your text cursor is at the edge of your page. Press the Tab key twice and then type County. Press Return.

The cursor should have lined up exactly under the word you have just typed; if not press the Tab key twice. Now type Hampshire, then press Return.

Complete your column of counties by adding the following: Devon, Somerset, Cornwall, Sussex, using the Tab key when necessary.

Your column should look like this:

> County
> Hampshire
> Devon
> Somerset
> Cornwall
> Sussex

Action 3

Make sure the cursor is at the edge of the page. Type the following heading: County. This time do not press Return but instead press the Tab key three times. Type:

County Town. There are now two headings. Now press Return. The cursor should be lined up exactly with the first heading so type: Essex.

Press the Tab key three times. The cursor lines up with the second heading.

Now type: Chelmsford. Complete the list so that it looks like the following:

County	County Town
Essex	Chelmsford
Dorset	Dorchester
Hertfordshire	Hertford
Oxfordshire	Oxford
Norfolk	Norwich

Section 21:
Margins

Essential Information

Margins are set automatically by the computer. The top and bottom margins are set at 2.54 cm and the left and right margins are set at 3.17 cm. Because these sizes are set automatically by the computer they are known as the default sizes. On occasion, however, you may wish to alter the margins in order to contain the text in a smaller or larger area of the page. The exercises below show you how to set the margins yourself.

Action 1

Open a new document. Go to **File** and click on **Page Setup** (Fig. 39).

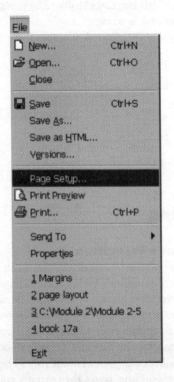

Fig. 39

Action 2

The **Page Setup** box is displayed (Fig. 40 and 40a). It has four tabs. Click once on the **Margins** tab.

Notice the default sizes are set in centimetres.

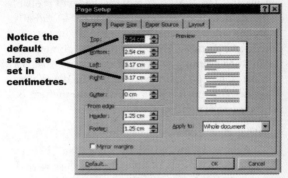

Fig. 40
Office 97

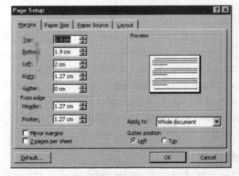

Fig. 40a

Action 3

Locate the two boxes labelled **Left** and **Right**. Within these boxes are shown the sizes of the margins in centimetres (cm). At the moment they will probably show the default sizes shown in Figures 40 and 40a.

By the side of the text boxes there are upward and downward pointing arrows. Move the pointer onto the upward pointing arrow by **Left** and increase 3.17 to 8 cm (if you go past the 8 cm, use the down arrow to reduce the number). Do the same to the text box for the right margin.

Action 4

Look at the **Preview** box on the right to see the effect of changing the numbers and therefore the size of the margins. The margin sizes that you have just chosen will have created a very narrow document!

Action 5

Reduce the left margin to 3 cm and the right margin to 3 cm. Look at the Preview box. The document is now much wider. As you would not wish at this stage to keep these altered margins, click on **Cancel** at the bottom of the box. When you do want to keep the margins that you have set, click on **OK** and the new sizes will be applied to the page.

Action 6

The same technique can be used to alter the sizes of the top and bottom margins.

Section 22:
Moving Text

Essential Information

The **Cut, Copy** and **Paste** buttons (Fig. 41) allow you to move text to different places on the page and between documents. Identify these functions on the Standard toolbar. Move the pointer onto each button without clicking. As it moves onto each, a label appears. This helps you to select the correct button that you wish to use.

Fig. 41

Action 1

Type a few lines of text. Highlight the first line. Now move the pointer onto the Cut button and click once. The first line disappears. Highlight the next line, move the pointer onto Cut and click once. Once again the line of text is removed. Carry on, removing the remainder of the text using the same procedure.

Action 2

Type a few lines of text. Highlight the first line. Move the pointer onto the button called Copy and click once.

Now move the pointer so that it is at the end of the last word of the last line of text and click once. Notice that the text cursor on the screen is pulsing in the spot where you have just clicked. Move the pointer to the Paste function on the toolbar and click once. Do not click on the picture of the paintbrush. There should now be a copy of the first line that you highlighted at the end of your piece of text.

This method can be used to highlight any part of the text and to copy it anywhere on the page or even to place it in another document.

Action 3

Type a few lines of text and highlight the first line. Click once on the Cut button. The line disappears.

Move the pointer to another part of the page and click once to move the text cursor into position. Now click on Paste and the copied line will appear in its new position.

Action 4

You may wish to make a duplication of the whole of your text. In this instance, use the Copy function rather than Cut.

Type a few lines of text. Highlight the whole document and then click on Copy. Now scroll down the page until you reach a clean part of the screen. If the cursor will not travel below your text, move the pointer to the end of the last word of the document, click once and the blinking text cursor will appear. Now press Return.

Click on the Paste button. There should now be two copies of the document.

Top Tip
It does take time to become proficient at the functions Cut, Copy and Paste, so keep practising.

Section 23:
Bullets and Numbering

Essential Information
It is possible to select various styles of numbering and bullets to suit different documents. Once your selection has been made it is then possible to include the bullets and numbering on your page by using the appropriate button on the toolbar. This allows you to decide where and when to use a bullet or a number. Microsoft Word will automatically insert a number or bullet every time you press Return. When you want to stop using this function, press Return twice or deactivate by clicking on the relevant button on the Formatting toolbar. First you need to select a style of bullets or numbers so follow the steps below.

Action 1

Click on **Format** on the menu bar. A drop-down menu appears. Click on **Bullets and Numbering** (Fig. 42).

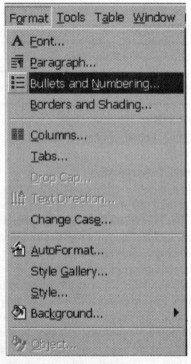

Fig. 42

Action 2

Notice that the Bullets and Numbering box that appears on the screen has three different tabs (Fig. 43). They are **Bulleted**, **Numbered** and **Outline Numbered**.

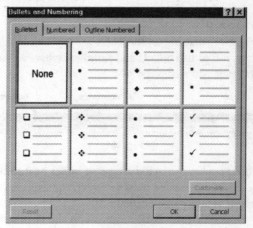

Fig. 43

Click on the tab **Bulleted**. As you can see from Figure 43, seven different styles of bullets are shown on the Bulleted tab. At the moment the box **None** is highlighted by a thick black border. This shows that at the moment no style of bullet has been selected. Click on the box next to **None** showing plain circular bullets.

Action 3

Notice that a thick line now highlights this box. Click on a different bullet box and notice that the highlight has moved again. Now choose a style that you prefer and then click on OK at the bottom of the box.

Action 4

On the Formatting toolbar there are two buttons that allow you to use bullets and numbers whenever and wherever you wish (Fig. 44).

Numbers   **Bullets**

Fig. 44

Once you have selected a type of bullet or number, these buttons can be used to switch the function on and off as and when needed.

Notice that the **Bullet** button on the Formatting toolbar is now depressed (Fig. 45).

Fig. 45

The **Number** button is not in use and is therefore not depressed. Notice the difference in appearance of the two buttons. To deactivate the Bullet button, click once on the Bullet button on the toolbar. Notice that the Bullet button is now no longer depressed. To reactivate the Bullet function, click once again on the Bullet button on the toolbar. Notice that a bullet has now appeared on your page.

Type next to the bullet: Dogs. Press Return. A new bullet has appeared. Type next to it: Cats. Press Return. Every time you press Return a bullet will appear. Type next to the third bullet: Horses.

Now add the following to the list: Ducks, Geese, Donkeys, Ponies. Remember to press the Return key after each word and a bullet will appear ready for the next word in the list.

Your list should look as follows but perhaps with your bullets in a different style:

- Dogs
- Cats
- Horses
- Ducks
- Geese
- Donkeys
- Ponies

Action 5
You are now going to remove the bullet function and select Numbered.

Go to **Format**, select **Bullets and Numbering** and select the tab entitled **Numbered**.

Seven style options appear. Click on any style.

Action 6

Look at the bottom of the box and identify the following:

⊙ Restart numbering   O Continue previous list

Make sure that **Restart numbering** (Fig. 46) has been selected: click on the circle and a black dot will appear in the centre, indicating selection.

Fig. 46

Click on OK, the box disappears and your page is ready for typing. Notice that the numbering button on the menu bar is now depressed. (If you wish to stop this function or the bullet function simply click once on the relevant button on the toolbar.) Your page is now ready for typing with automatic numbering. This works in the same manner as using bullets: whenever you press Return a number will be placed on the page. To remove any unwanted numbers that may appear, or if you make a mistake, position the cursor in the correct place and then press Backspace to delete.

Section 24:
Find and Replace

Essential Information
Find and Replace enables you to save time in replacing one word within your text with a different one. It is useful if you have repeatedly misspelt a word or need to find a particular word in a long document.

Action 1
Click on **Edit**. On the drop-down menu that appears click on **Find** (Fig. 47).

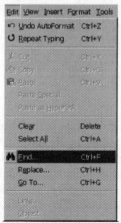

Fig. 47

Action 2

The **Find and Replace** box is displayed. Notice that it has three tabs at the top: **Find**, **Replace**, and **Go To**. Click on **Replace** (Fig. 48).

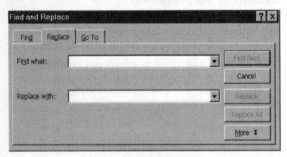

Fig. 48

Notice that the **Replace** tab has two text boxes: **Find what** and **Replace with**.

Action 3

In the **Find what** box, type in the word that you wish to be removed and in the **Replace with** box, type in the replacement word. Click on the **Replace** button and the program searches and highlights an example of the word. Read the sentence to make sure that the new word makes sense, click on **Replace** and the word is replaced with the alternative. If you do not wish a word to be replaced, click on **Find next** and that example will be ignored and the program will move onto the next.

Action 4

If you don't wish to go through all the text looking at each word individually, you can replace all the examples of the unwanted word by clicking on **Replace all**. Below are two examples of how to use **Find and Replace**.

Example 1

Open a new document and type the following:

> We all know that apples are good for us but not many people are aware that apples are also members of the plum family.

You need to replace the word apples with the word damsons. In the **Find what** box, type in the word 'apples'. In the **Replace with** box, type the word 'damsons'. Click on **Replace**. This will search the document for the first example of the word 'apples' and highlight it. To replace the word, click on **Replace** on the right of the box.

When the computer has finished searching the document, the box below will appear.

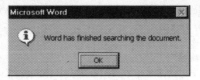

Fig. 49

Click on **OK**. Click on Close on the **Find and Replace** window.

Example 2

If you wish to replace *all* the examples of a certain word, the computer can replace them all at the same time. However, you must be certain that you really do want to change all the words. If you are in any doubt, change the required words one by one so that you can read the sentence before making the change.

Type the following:

> Two and two are four. Five and six are
> eleven. Nine and ten are nineteen.
> Three and one are four whilst seven and
> thirteen are twenty.

Click on **Edit**, **Find** and on the tab **Replace**. Type the word 'and' in the **Find what** text box and type 'plus' in the **Replace with** text box. Click on **Replace all** on the right of the box. Check your text to see if the computer has completed its task.

Section 25:
Minimise, Maximise and Restore

Essential Information

These are functions that alter the size of pages, enabling you to work on several at once. They are used all the time in word processing so do take a little time to become comfortable using them.

In the top right-hand corner of the Microsoft Word window you will have one of these two sets of boxes:

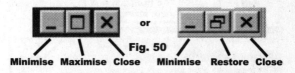

Minimise Maximise Close   Minimise Restore Close

Fig. 50

Office 97 has sizing boxes for each window whilst Office 2000 and Works 2000 combine the window and the program into one. If you have Office 97 look at Action 1 and for Office 2000 and Works 2000 go to Action 2.

Action 1

Look at the right-hand corner of the **page** and the Word **program** and you will see that they both have a set of these boxes.

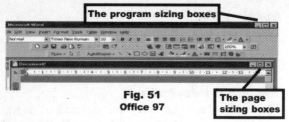

Fig. 51
Office 97

Now go on to Action 3.

Action 2

On Office and Works 2000 there are only sizing boxes on the **Program** window and the page has just a Close box (Fig. 52).

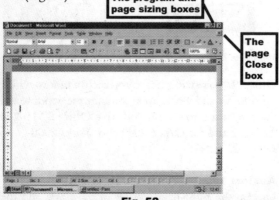

Fig. 52
Office and Works 2000

Now go on to Action 3.

Action 3

To Maximise or Restore, use the **page** sizing boxes in Office 97 and the **program** sizing boxes for Office 2000 and Works 2000.

Your page or program may show either 2 or 1 boxes in the centre of the three boxes.

If it shows 2 (Restore), click on it once and watch what happens. Look closely at the centre box. It should now show 1 (Maximise).

If it shows 1 (Maximise), click on it once and watch what happens. Look closely at the centre box. It should now show 2 (Restore).

If you are using Office 97 go on to read Action 4 and for Office 2000 and Works 2000 read Action 5.

Action 4 (Office 97)

Click once on the Minimise button. Your page shrinks into a small bar across the bottom of the screen.

To restore the window or page, click once on the Restore button on the small bar. The window may be restored immediately, or a menu will appear (Fig. 53), in which case click once on either of the Restore buttons.

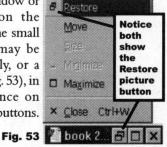

Notice both show the Restore picture button

Fig. 53

Action 5 (Office 2000 and Works 2000)

Click on the Minimise button and the whole window will shrink down to a button on the taskbar (Fig. 54). It is possible to open up a number of documents and then minimise them so that they sit on the taskbar and are thus easy to recall when you need them, especially during the process of copying from one document to another.

Fig. 54

To Restore the document to the screen, simply click on the document button on the taskbar.

Action 6

You can also make a window larger or smaller by using the pointer. Move the pointer to the left-hand side of the window frame. Move it so that it sits right on the edge. The moment that it does sit on the edge, the arrow will change to a double-headed arrow.

Now click on the left-hand mouse button, hold down the button and drag the pointer to the right to halfway across the screen. As you drag the pointer, you will also drag the outside frame of the window.

Release the button. The window will now be reduced to half the screen.

Action 7

Place the pointer back on the edge of the left-hand side of the window and click and drag the window back into the original position.

Top Tip

Click on Maximise and the window will expand. Click on Restore and the window will reduce down to a smaller size.

Section 26:
Toolbars

Essential Information

Toolbars list utilities and functions for different programs. Open a new page in Word. Look at the top of the screen and as well as the menu bar there will probably be the Standard toolbar and the Formatting toolbar, all of which you have been using throughout this book. There may be other toolbars also visible: there are many that can be used for various purposes. It is very easy to mislay a toolbar, so don't panic if you lose one.

Action 1

To find the toolbars, go to View on the menu bar. Click once and highlight Toolbars on the drop-down menu. A list of different toolbars appears in another drop-down menu. The ones that are currently displayed will have a tick by the side of them (Fig. 55).

Fig. 55

Choose a toolbar that has not been ticked and click on it once. A new toolbar will appear on your screen.

Action 2

To remove the extra toolbar, go to **View** and click once. Select **Toolbars** and click once to remove the tick by the toolbar that you wish to remove. Look at the screen and the toolbar will have disappeared. Make sure that you retain the Standard and Formatting bars.

Top Tip

Remember, if you appear to have lost a toolbar, go to **View** then **Toolbars** and make sure that the relevant toolbar has a tick against it.

Action 3

You can move toolbars around the screen. Look at the left-hand side of the Standard, Formatting and Menu bars at the top of your page. On the grey strip there appears to be two raised grey lines at the very edge of the strip. By placing your cursor on these grey strips and using the method of click and drag it is possible to move the toolbars and menu bar to other areas of the screen.

Figures 56 and 57 show the toolbars that have been moved onto the centre of the screen.

Fig. 56
Office 97

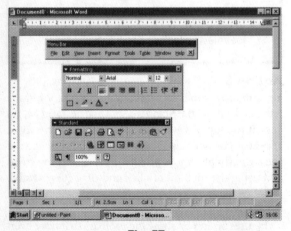

Fig. 57
Office 2000 and Works 2000

Action 4

Place your cursor on the raised lines of the menu bar, keeping your finger down on the left mouse button, and drag the menu bar down onto the screen. Release the mouse button.

Go back to the top of the page and repeat the procedure with the Standard and Formatting toolbars, placing each of them onto your screen, as shown in the picture above.

Action 5

To replace the toolbars, place your cursor on the blue strip of the menu bar.

Click once and, holding the button down, drag the bar back to the top of the screen.

Wait until the bar becomes thinner and more elongated and then release the button. The menu bar should now be back in its correct place.

Repeat this procedure and replace the Standard and Formatting bars.

Section 27:
Copying Between Documents

Essential Information

One of the most useful aspects of Cut, Copy and Paste is being able to copy from one document to another. It is in this process that knowing how to minimise and restore a page is essential. Refer back to Section 25 for how to Minimise and Restore.

Remember, if you are using Office 2000 or Works 2000 you will only have one set of sizing boxes.

Action 1 (Office 97)

When you are copying between documents you need to minimise the page and not the program. The page buttons are the lowest three boxes (Fig. 58).

Fig. 58

Now read Action 2.

Action 2

Open up a new document and type one line of text.
Now open another new document and type two lines
of text. Highlight the two lines of text on this second
document and then click on the **Copy** button on the
toolbar.

Action 3

Minimise the second document. It will contract into
a button at the bottom of the screen (Office 97) or
onto the taskbar (Office 2000 and Works 2000).

Action 4

Place the text cursor at the end of the line on the first
document and then move the pointer onto the **Paste**
button on the toolbar and click once.

The lines from the second document will have been
added to the line on the first document, thus
combining the text of the two documents. In this way
you can add sections of information from one
document to another.

Section 28:
Word Templates and Wizards

Essential Information

Word templates and Wizards are preformatted sample documents that take the hard work out of deciding how to set out a particular type of document. The Wizard leads you through various stages to complete the template. The **Memo** and the **Envelope Wizard**, for example, will help you create correctly formatted and well laid out memos and envelopes. There are many different types of templates available. All you have to do is replace the sample text with your text. The templates on Office 97 have been included in Office 2000 and Works 2000, which have an extended range.

Action 1

For Office 97 and 2000, open Word in the usual way, click once on **File** on the menu bar and then click on **New** (Fig. 59). For Works 2000, open a blank document, click once on **File** on the menu bar and then click on **New** and then on **More Word Templates** (Fig. 59a).

Fig. 59
Office 97 and 2000

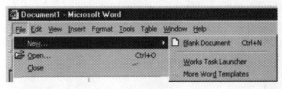

Fig. 59a
Works 2000

Action 2

A box will open displaying a number of tabs with a variety of headings (Works does not have the tab called Business Planner Template). Click on each of the tabs and see the variety of templates available.

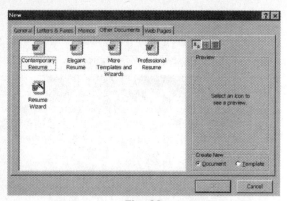

Fig. 60
Office 97

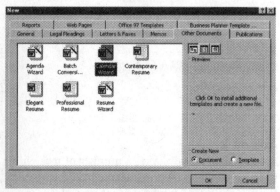

Fig. 60a
Office 2000

Figure 60a shows that Office 2000 has a greater number of tabs and templates.

Action 3

When you have found a template that suits your purpose, simply click on the icon, make sure that the radio button called **Create New Document** is activated and then click on **OK**. The Wizard will lead you through the process. That's all there is to it!

Action 4

Look at Figure 61. It is an example of a simple template for a company letter. As you can see, all you have to do is click on the page and replace the existing words and information with your own.

[CLICK **HERE** AND TYPE COMPANY NAME]

September 27, 2001

[Click **here** and type recipient's address]

Dear Sir or Madam:

Type your letter here. For more details on modifying this letter template, double-click ⊠. To return to this letter, use the Window menu.

Sincerely,

[Click **here** and type your name]
[Click **here** and type job title]

Fig. 61

On Works 2000 there are task templates. Click once on **Tasks** on the black bar at the top of Works Task Launcher or if you are already in Word, go to **File**, click **New** and select **Works Task Launcher**. On the left is a range of tasks. Click on one of the tasks and in the panel to the right of the tasks are listed all the various templates within that subject. For example, in Figure 62, the subject highlighted is Letters and Labels, and to the right are all the templates within that category. Click on whichever one you want and the Wizard will lead you through the procedure.

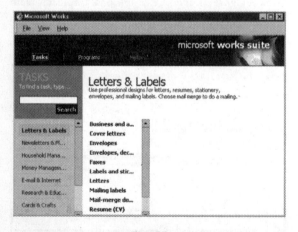

Fig. 62
Microsoft Works

Section 29:
Saving a Document

Once you have created a document you will probably wish to save it in order to work on at a later date or to keep as a reference. It is possible to save documents onto various parts of the computer but it is easier to keep control if they are saved onto a floppy disk or into the folder called My Documents, which is on the computer's hard disk.

Action 1 (Saving into My Documents)
Once you have created a document that you wish to save you must first decide upon a name to give it.

Action 2
Go to **File** on the menu bar and click once. The File drop-down menu appears. Move your pointer down the list until it highlights **Save As** (Fig. 63) Click once.

Fig. 63

A **Save As** box appears. Figure 64 shows the **Save As** box for Office 97 and Figure 65 for Office 2000 and Works 2000.

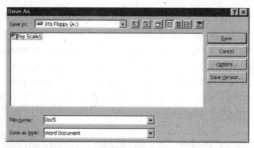

Fig. 64
Office 97

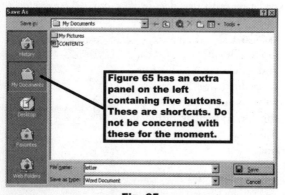

Figure 65 has an extra panel on the left containing five buttons. These are shortcuts. Do not be concerned with these for the moment.

Fig. 65
Office 2000
Works 2000

Action 3

Notice that on both Figure 64 and Figure 65 there are four white text boxes. The largest text box shows the names of documents that have been previously saved.

Action 4

Each of the three narrow text boxes has a down arrow at one end. Click on the down arrow on the first text box called **Save in** (Fig. 66). A drop-down list is displayed showing the possible places to save a document. It is important to look at this box before you save, as you need to know exactly where you are saving a document. The My Documents folder is held on the hard drive which is represented by **C**. Move the pointer down the drop-down list, highlight **C** and click once (Fig. 66).

Fig. 66

Action 5

In the large text box are all the programs and files (including My Documents) held on C (Fig. 67).

Fig. 67

Highlight and double-click on **My Documents**. My Documents will now be inserted into the **Save in** text box. On Office 2000 and Works 2000, the button on the left-hand panel will also perform the same function. Click on the button and My Documents will appear in the **Save in** text box (Fig. 68).

Fig. 68

Top Tip

To help keep your files organised, your document could be saved into a personal folder contained within My Documents (e.g. Fred's Box, as shown in Fig. 68). To know more about how to create and use folders, see *Chapter Seven: How to Create and Manage Files.*

Action 6

Look at the third text box called **File name**. This will show the name that the computer has chosen for your document. Usually this will be the very first words of the document. If you wish to select a different name for the document, click once in the text box and the text cursor will appear. You can remove the name the computer has chosen and type in the new name for the document.

Action 7

The fourth text box is called **Save as type**. Click on the arrow by the side of this text box and you will notice that there are a range of formats that can be selected. While you are working on word documents, select **Word Documents** for this box, as shown in Figure 69.

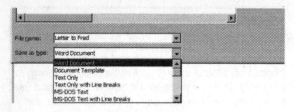

Fig. 69

Action 8

Once you have typed in the name that you have chosen for your document into the third text box, click on the **Save** button, which for Office 97 is set on the top right side of the box and for Office 2000 and Works 2000 is at the bottom. Your document will now have been saved into My Documents.

If you decide that you do not wish to save yet, remove the **Save in** box by clicking once on **Cancel**.

Top Tip
It's a good idea to practise the above.
Don't worry if you can't remember it off by heart just yet, it takes time to learn this procedure.

Saving on Floppy Disk

Essential Information

If you do not know how to load a floppy disk, refer to page 186. Saving work onto a floppy disk involves almost the same procedure as saving into My Documents. The following actions will lead you through the process.

Action 1

Create a document that you want to save (just a few lines will do for you to practise).

Action 2

Insert the floppy disk into the floppy drive in the systems unit.

Action 3

Go to **File** on the menu bar and click once. The File drop-down menu appears. Move your pointer down the list until it highlights **Save As** and click once (Fig. 70).

Fig. 70

The same **Save As** box appears as shown in Section 29, Figures 64 and 65.

Action 4

Click on the down arrow on the first text box called **Save in** (Fig. 71) and the drop-down list appears. Highlight and click on **3½ Floppy** which will then be inserted into the text box.

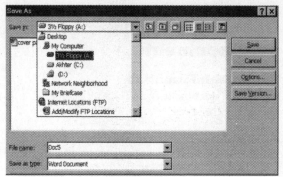

Fig. 71

Look at the third text box called **File Name** and remove the computer's selection by using backspace or delete and type in the new name for the document.

Action 5

In the fourth text box called **Save As Type**, select **Word Document**.

Action 6

Click on the **Save** button, which for Office 97 is set on the top right side of the box and for Office 2000 and Works 2000 is at the bottom. Your document will now have been saved onto your floppy disk.

If you decide that you do not wish to save yet, remove the box by clicking once on **Cancel**.

Section 30:
Opening a Document from My Documents

Essential Information

Opening a document is a very similar operation to saving a document.

Action 1

Click on **File** on the menu bar and scroll down until you reach the word **Open**.

Click once and the **Open** box is displayed (Figs. 72 and 73). Office 97 (Fig. 73) has a few more text boxes than Office 2000 and Works 2000 (Fig. 72). The ones we are concerned with are the two narrow boxes called **Look in** and **File of type** and the large white text box which displays contents.

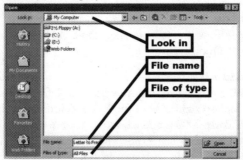

Fig. 72
Works 2000 and Office 2000

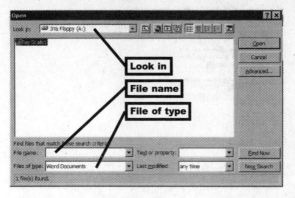

Fig. 73
Office 97

Action 2

Click on the down arrow by the text box called **Files of type** and make sure that **Word Documents** is selected (or All files).

Action 3

Click on the down arrow by the text box called **Look in**, and a drop-down menu will appear (Fig. 74). Move the pointer onto **C** so that it is highlighted and click once.

Fig. 74

Action 4

In the large text box the contents of **C** will now be displayed, including My Documents (Fig. 75).

Fig. 75

Click on **My Documents** so that it is highlighted and click on the **Open** button. The contents of My Documents will be shown, including the document that you have saved.

Top Tip
Office 2000 and Works 2000 Shortcut
By clicking on the My Documents button on the left-hand panel you will be taken straight into the My Documents folder.

Action 5

Move the pointer onto the name of the document that you wish to open and click once so that it is highlighted in blue (Fig. 76). Click on **Open**. Your document will now appear on the screen.

Fig. 76

Section 31:
Opening a Document from a Floppy Disk

Essential Information

Opening a document from a floppy disk is the same procedure as opening from My Documents. Just remember to insert the floppy disk into the floppy drive (p.186)!

Action 1

Click on **File** on the menu bar and scroll down until you reach the word **Open**. Click once and the **Open** box is displayed.

Action 2

In the **Look in** text box, click on the down arrow and a drop-down list will appear.

Action 3

Move the pointer onto **3½ Floppy**, so that it is highlighted (Fig. 77) and then click once.

Action 4

The large text box will now display the contents of the floppy.

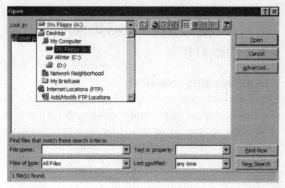

Fig. 77

Action 5

Click on the arrow by the text box called **Files of type** and make sure that you select **Word Document** (or All Files).

Action 6

Move the pointer onto the name of the document that you wish to open and click once, so that it is highlighted in blue. Click on the word **Open**. Your document will now appear on the screen.

Section 32:
The Standard Toolbar: Shortcuts

Essential Information

The Standard toolbar, like the Formatting toolbar, is set at the top of the Word window and carries a number of features that are shortcuts to functions that you have already met. There are also other buttons that allow you to move text, preview your work, check for mistakes and undo any mistakes.

There are shortcuts to opening a new document, a file and to saving.

Action 1

Look at the first three pictures on the Standard toolbar. Then look at the drop-down menu from File on the menu bar. These pictures are repeated, along with the name of the function.

Fig. 78
Standard toolbar

Action 2

Look for the word **New** and the small picture of a new page on the File drop-down menu. Look on the Standard toolbar and find the same picture. This is the shortcut. Click once to open a new page.

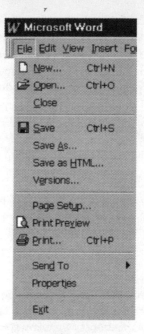

Fig. 79
File drop-down menu

Action 3

Look on the File drop-down menu and find the word
Open. Look on the Standard toolbar and find the same
picture of the open yellow folder. Click once on the
folder and the normal open box appears on the screen.

131

Action 4

Look at the File drop-down menu and find the word **Save**. Locate the same picture on the Standard toolbar. This is a shortcut to saving a document. There are two points to remember about this shortcut:

1. If it is the first time that the document has been saved, the **Save As** box will appear on the screen as normal.

2. If the document has been previously saved it will automatically save it again into the same place. The **Save As** box will not appear. So if you wish to save your document into a different location, do not use the Save button on the Standard toolbar.

Action 5

There are two other quick ways of opening a recent file. If you are already in Word, click on **File** and at the bottom of the drop-down menu you will see a list of the most recently opened documents. Single-click on the name of the document to open it.

Another quick route is through the Start menu. Click once on **Start** and move the pointer onto **Documents**. A list of recently opened files will appear. Click on the file you wish to open.

Section 33:
Print Preview

Essential Information

Print Preview allows a document to be viewed before time and paper is wasted in printing. It gives you the opportunity to discover any errors that may exist and to correct them before printing. It also enables you to see how well you have set out the text, so it's a good idea to get into the habit of previewing your work as you go along.

Action 1

Open up a page of previously saved work or a blank page. Go to **File** on the menu bar and click once. Click once on **Print Preview** on the drop-down menu (Fig. 80).

Fig. 80

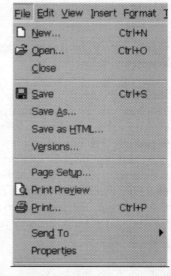

Move the pointer onto the page on the screen and you will notice that the arrow becomes a magnifying glass. Click once and the page becomes enlarged. Click again and the page is returned to its previous size.

Action 2

Look at the Print Preview toolbar (Fig. 81).

Fig. 81

On the screen, locate the buttons **Multiple Pages**, **Zoom** and **Close**.

Action 3

Move the pointer to the **Multiple Pages** button and click once. You now have a choice of how many pages to preview (Fig. 82).

Move the pointer over the grid. You will notice that as the pointer moves, pages on the grid are highlighted. Highlight two pages on the grid and click once. Notice that the single page has moved to the left to allow room for a second page. In this way you can view up to six pages at once.

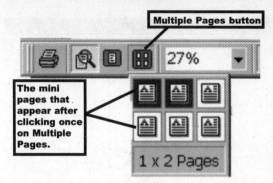

Fig. 82

Action 4

Fig. 83
The Zoom button

The **Zoom** function (Fig. 83) allows you to increase and decrease the size of the page whilst in preview. Notice that the Zoom function is showing a percentage. This is the percentage size of the page whilst in preview.

Notice that to the right of the Zoom button there is a down arrow.

Action 5

Click once on the down arrow and a drop-down list showing percentages is displayed (Fig. 84).

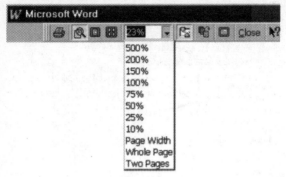

Fig. 84

Click on 10% and you will see that the page really does shrink! Now go back to the Zoom function and click on 50% and see how the page increases.

Action 6

Click on **Close** on the preview toolbar and you are returned to the normal page.

You cannot make changes to the document whilst in Print Preview so if any need to be made you must always return to the normal page.

You should always save your document to preserve any changes that you have made.

Section 34:
Preparing To Print

Essential Information
Make sure that the printer is connected to the set-up and that it is switched on and loaded with paper. Before printing you need to ensure that the computer knows what size of paper is being used and which way round the page should be. This is done through **Page Setup**.

Action 1
Go to **File** on the menu bar and click once. On the drop-down menu, click on **Page Setup** (Fig. 85).

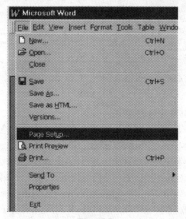

Fig. 85

137

Action 2

A box opens called **Page Setup** (Fig. 86). Notice that it has four tabs. Make sure that you select the tab called **Paper Size**.

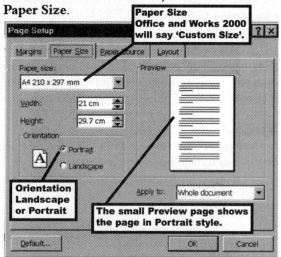

Fig. 86
Office 97

Action 3

Under the title **Paper Size**, the text box has a down arrow. If you click on this a drop-down list will display the various paper sizes. For this exercise we will assume that you will be using A4 paper in your printer, so click on A4 210 x 297 mm (click on **Custom Size** for Office and Works 2000).

Action 4

Under **Orientation** you will see that you can choose whether to print in landscape or portrait. Click on the radio button to choose **Landscape**. Notice that the small preview page on the right now shows the page in landscape style.

Now click on **Portrait**. The preview page has changed to a portrait style. This facility allows you greater flexibility in designing your documents.

Action 5

Now that you have completed the Page Setup you can go on to print.

Section 35:
Printing

Action 1

Go to **File** on the menu bar and click once.
A drop-down menu appears (Fig. 87). Click once on Print.

Fig. 87

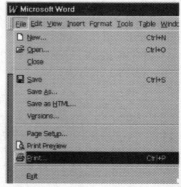

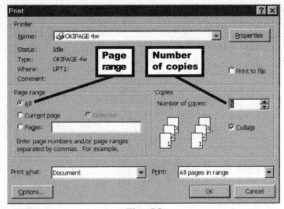

Fig. 88

Action 2

The Print box appears with various options. Look at **Page Range**. You have a choice of what to print:

All: If you choose this option all the pages of your document will be printed.

Current page: This option means that only the page that is currently visible on the screen will be printed.

Pages: This option allows you to select certain pages within the document. When you choose this option you will need to type in the page numbers you wish to print in the pages text box. The printer will then only print those pages that you have selected.

When you have decided on which pages you wish to print, click on the relevant radio button or type in the page range in the text box. For example, 3,5,9 or 1-50.

Action 3
On the right-hand side of the Print box is a section to select the number of copies that you want. The small upward pointing arrow will allow you to increase the number in the copies text box, whilst the downward pointing arrow will reduce the number. Alternatively, you can click on the text box and type in the number of copies that you wish to print.

Action 4
Once you have selected the page size, orientation and number of copies, click on **OK** and the printing will begin. If you change your mind and do not wish to print at this stage, click on **Cancel**.

Action 5
There is a printing shortcut on the Standard toolbar (Fig. 89). It is the same picture of a printer found on the drop-down menu from File. Only use this printer button when you have already set up your page and only require one copy of one document.

Print   **Fig. 89**

The Beginner's Guide to Computers and the Internet

Chapter Three:
How to Use Microsoft Help

Section 1:
Using Microsoft Help

Essential Information
Microsoft Help is available in every Microsoft program. The Help system is comprehensive, easy to use and context sensitive. You will find a Help button on the menu bar of most windows and boxes that you use. Help can also be found on the Start menu.

JARGON BUSTER
Context sensitive
Relating to the operation being carried out.

Top Tip
Do make a conscious effort to use Help – it is an excellent way of extending your knowledge and increasing your confidence. Look on it as a built-in manual that will enable you to discover more about your PC programs.

Section 2:
Help Topics in Windows Help

Action 1
Help Topics: Windows Help can be accessed from the Start menu (see Fig. 1),

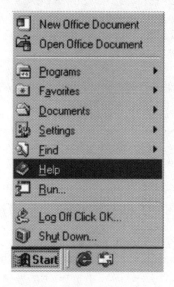

Fig. 1
Help on the Start menu

or from the Help button on the menu bar of a window (Fig. 2).

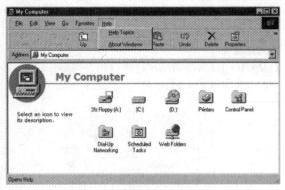

Fig. 2
Help button

When the **Help Topics** box is displayed you will notice that there are three tabs (Fig. 3).

Action 2

Click on the **Contents** tab and you will see a group of files shown as books. By clicking on a book, the contents will appear, and by clicking on a particular subject an expanded explanation will be displayed.

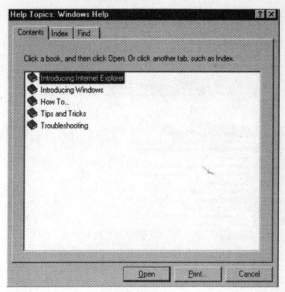

Fig. 3

Action 3

Click on the **Index** tab (Fig. 4). Type the first few letters of the subject that you need help with into the text box and a list of contents will appear in the box below. Click on a relevant subject, click **Display** and if you wish to keep a paper copy, click once on **Print**.

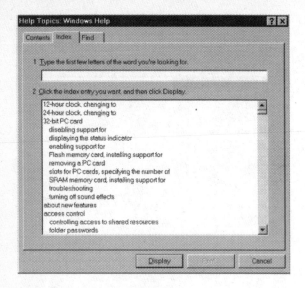

Fig. 4

Action 4

The **Find** tab will enable you to search for specific words and phrases in Help Topics. Click on the tab and the **Find Setup Wizard** will appear (Fig. 5). Read the information on the Wizard, then click **Next>** and follow the instructions as they appear.

Fig. 5

Section 3:
What's This?

Essential Information
This is a very useful tool, especially for beginners. It acts as a reminder of various functions and features.

Action 1
What's This? can be found on the Help button on Office 97 and Office 2000 (Fig. 6).

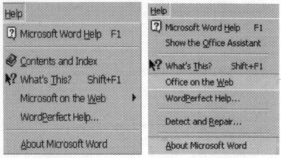

Office 97	Office 2000

Fig. 6

What's This? can also be found on some boxes by clicking on the question mark in the top right-hand corner of the box (see Fig. 7).

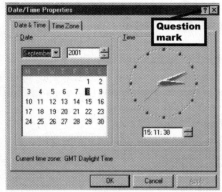

Fig. 7

When you have accessed What's This? you will find that the pointer changes into a cursor with a question mark attached (Fig. 8). This is called a 'point and tell' system.

Fig. 8
What's This?

Section 4:
Using What's This? on Boxes

Follow this example to see how using What's This? on boxes works in practise.

Action 1

Open the **Control Panel** (go to My Computer and double-click on Control Panel) and double-click on the **Date/ Time** icon. Click on the question mark in the top right-hand corner (Fig. 9).

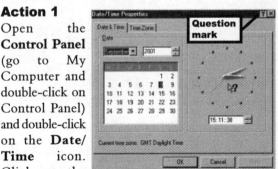

Fig. 9

Action 2

Move the cursor (in the shape of a question mark) across the screen on to the clock face, click once and a yellow explanation box will appear (Fig. 10).

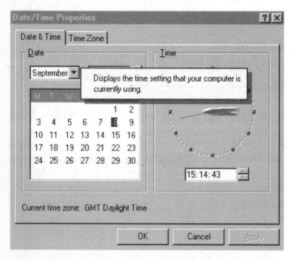

Fig. 10

After you have read the explanation, remove the explanation box on it by clicking once on the box. Close the Date/Time Properties box and the Control Panel and My Computer windows by clicking on the Close box.

Section 5:
Using What's This? within Office 97, 2000 and Word Processing on Works 2000

Essential Information

This is exactly the same as using What's This? on boxes within windows.

Follow this example to see how using What's This? in word processing works in practise.

Action 1

Open your word processing program. If you are not sure about how to do this, refer to *Chapter Two: How to use Word Processing*, Section 2.

Action 2

Click on the Help button on the menu bar and select What's This? (See Fig. 11.)

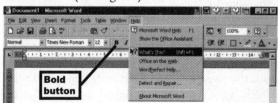

Fig. 11

Move the pointer across the screen and click once on the Bold button (Fig. 12).

Fig. 12

Read the explanation and then remove it by clicking on the yellow box.

Action 3
Close Word by clicking on the cross in the Close box.

Section 6:
Help and the Office Assistant

Essential Information
The **Office Assistant** helps you solve problems by enabling you to ask a direct question. The Office Assistant can be called up by clicking on the Help button on the menu bar or by clicking on the question mark (Fig. 13) in the top right-hand corner of the window (Fig. 12).

Fig. 13

Action 1

Open the Assistant by one of the methods above and a text box with the phrase 'Type your question here' will appear. Delete these words and type in your question. Click once on 'Search' and possible answers will be displayed.

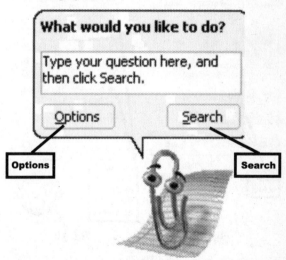

Fig. 14
Office Assistant called Clippit

In Figure 15, the Office Assistant shows the first five results of a search about italicising. By clicking on **See more**, another five results are listed (Fig. 16).

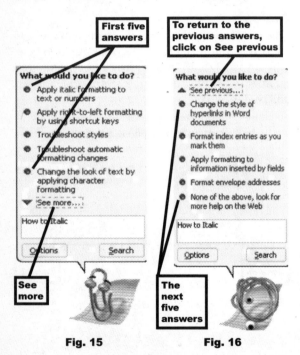

Fig. 15   **Fig. 16**

Action 2
To view an answer, double-click on a relevant item.

Section 7:
Show or Hide the Office Assistant

It is possible to hide the Office Assistant so that it only appears at your invitation. It can be recalled at your command by following Action 2.

Action 1
To hide the Office Assistant, click on the Help button and select **Hide the Office Assistant** from the drop-down menu (Fig. 17).

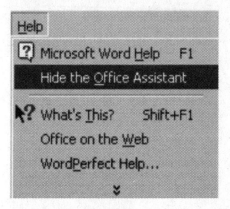

Fig. 17

Action 2

To show the Office Assistant, return to the Help button and click on **Show Office Assistant** on the drop-down menu (Fig. 18).

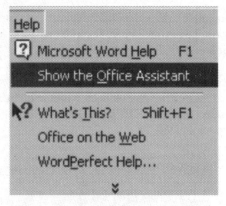

Fig. 18

Section 8:
Changing the Office Assistant

Action 1

To view the different Office Assistants, click once on **Help** on the menu bar, select **Show the Office Assistant**, click once on the **Options** button and then click once on the tab called **Gallery**. The various Office Assistants will be displayed as you click on **Next>** (Fig. 19). When you find one that you like, click on **OK** and your new selection will replace Clippit.

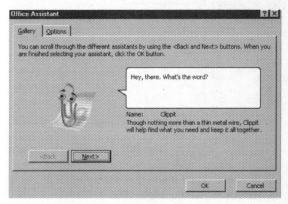

Fig. 19

Section 9:
Microsoft Help: Works Suite 2000

Action 1

Locate and click once on the **Help** button on the main window of Microsoft Works Suite (Fig. 20).

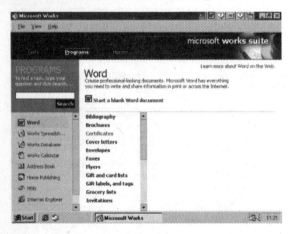

Fig. 20

On the drop-down menu that will appear, click once on **Microsoft Works Help** (Fig. 21).

The Works Task Launcher table of contents is then displayed (Fig. 22).

Action 2

You now have a choice of where to go. By clicking on **Get Help**, a list of various options will be displayed and you can choose what type of help you require.

Action 3

By clicking on the **Index** icon you will be presented with an alphabetical list of subjects held on Help (Fig. 23). Scroll down the page and find the item in which you are interested and then double-click on it. In the box below will be displayed those topics

Fig. 21

Fig. 22

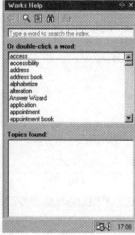

Fig. 23

appertaining to that particular subject. Alternatively, type in the first word of a topic in the top text box and they will appear listed in the bottom box. Select an item and double-click to view the information it offers.

Action 4

To close Works Help, click on the cross in the Close box in the top right-hand corner.

Section 10:
Microsoft Help on the Web

Additional help can be found by connecting directly to Microsoft via the web.

To do this, click on **Help** on the menu bar. If you have Office 97 then select **Microsoft Help on the Web** (Fig. 6) or if you have Office 2000 or Works 2000 then select **Office on the Web** (Fig. 6) and follow the instructions given.

Chapter Four:
How to Play Computer Games

Section 1:
Computer Games and Your PC

Essential Information

Your PC will already hold four computer games from Microsoft. These can be easily played and are simple to use (Section 2). However, to play some of the more sophisticated games you need to ensure that your system has the necessary equipment and accessories.

Some games take up a large amount of computer memory so check your PC's RAM. Broadly speaking, the newer the game, the larger the amount of PC memory they require. To play some of the more basic games your system should have at least 8 MB RAM. If you want to play the newest games, you should aim for 256 MB RAM.

In order to run games your system will also require a suitable graphics card. Initially the graphics card already in your PC will be adequate. However, as you gain in expertise and experience you may wish to upgrade to a new graphics card with its own processor. This will have the effect of making the games more realistic and faster.

If you are unsure about any of these aspects, contact your retailer or a computer engineer to advise you.

There are three different types of computer games: standard Microsoft games already loaded onto your PC, games on CD or DVD, and games on the Internet.

Section 2:
Standard Microsoft Games

Essential Information

There are four games on the Microsoft menu: Solitaire, FreeCell, Minesweeper and Hearts. They form a good introduction to how some of the less complex games are played. To play Solitaire see *Chapter One, Section 12.* Click once on **Start** on the taskbar, move your pointer to **Programs** then **Accessories** then **Games** and click on one of the four games listed.

Freecell

The object of this game is to move all four suites in their correct numerical order into the spaces in the top right corner. Click on **Help** for more on how to play this game.

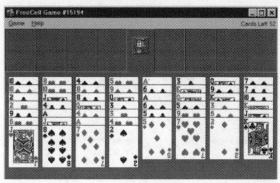

Fig. 1
Freecell

Minesweeper

The object of this game is to achieve the maximum number of points before being blown up! Click on **Help** for more information on how to play.

Fig. 2
Minesweeper

163

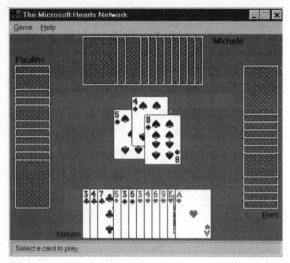

Fig. 3
Hearts

Hearts

To start this game, click on **Game** and select **New**.
The object is to lose all your cards by scoring the lowest
number of points. For more on how to play click on
Help.

```
          JARGON BUSTER
             Freebies
Free software available to download from the Internet.
```

Section 3:
Games on CD or DVD

Essential Information

An enormous number of games of varying degrees of complexity are available on CD and DVD. They range from traditional board games to the very latest 3D video-like adventures.

These can be as diverse as anything produced by the film industry: from spy thrillers and mystery to sci-fi and fantasy.

You can role-play by visiting historical battle scenes, drive a steam train, or save the world from aliens!

Games are controlled on the screen by the mouse or, if you prefer, you can use joysticks, gamepads or steering wheels. These are accessories which can be obtained from any computer or department store.

They are plugged into the game port of the systems unit and provide precision control and the use of action buttons. They also come with a CD-ROM which tells the computer that you have attached a new piece of hardware.

Action 1
Ensure that your system has enough memory. Always check the game's packaging for the size of memory required in order to avoid overloading the system.

Action 2
Connect your joystick, gamepad or steering wheel to the game port and make sure that you have run the accompanying CD-ROM so that the computer is aware of the new hardware.

Action 3
Load the game CD or DVD into the correct tray in the usual way and then follow the instructions. If you have problems in running the CD or DVD, refer to *Chapter Five: How to use Disks.*

Top Tip
Be Sociable!
Instead of the computer being the opponent, use a pair of gamepads or joysticks to compete against friends and family.

Section 4:
Game Developers

Most game developers have their own web sites that give previews and information about the games that they have on offer. (You can return to this chapter when you have read the chapters on how to use the Internet.) Here are a few games sites that you may find interesting:

http://www.novalogic.com   http://www.ubisoft.com
http://www.gameactive.net   http://www.lucasarts.com
          http://www.microsoft.com/games/

There are many more available that you can find with the help of a search engine.

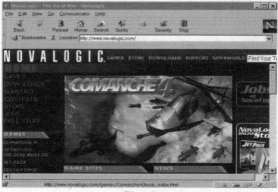

Fig. 4
The NovaLogic games site.

Section 5:
Games on the Internet

Essential Information

Many games can be downloaded from the Internet. It is possible to obtain some for free and others are available on a trial basis. Then if you don't like it, you don't have to buy it.

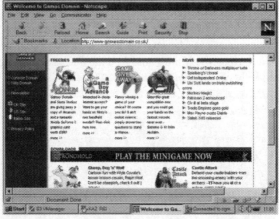

Fig. 5

This site (www.gamesdomain.co.uk) lists freebies and other downloads available.

There are three ways of playing online: against the computer, against another player, or against a group of players. Companies such as Microsoft and Virgin run games sites where you can link up with others to play your chosen game. There are a large number of games sites now available for children, like the Bonus SuperSite at www.bonus.com.

Fig. 6
The Bonus SuperSite

By clicking on Board Games (second from left, bottom row) the following page was downloaded, showing a number of traditional games.

Fig. 7

By clicking on to the link you gain access to the game.

The links below will help to get you started on Internet games. You could also use a search engine or directory to find other sites. Simply type 'computer games' into the text box and click 'Find'.

http://www.bonus.com
http://www.games.com
http://www.gamesdomain.com

JARGON BUSTER
Cheats

These are articles, magazines and books written about how to play certain games and the best way to win! They detail shortcuts to becoming more proficient at games on the market. Many games sites on the Internet also have a section called 'Cheats'. Look out for them when you pay the site a visit.

Section 6:
Games Magazines

Essential Information
There are a variety of magazines dedicated to playing games on the computer. Have a look at http:// www.pcgamer.co.uk as an example of what is on offer.

Section 7:
Have a Go before you Buy

If you are completely new (a newbie) to computer games, then a good way of getting an introduction to them is to visit a large department or computer store where there will usually be systems already set up with games for you to try out. You can also test a variety of accessories such as joysticks and steering wheels and get some idea of how they work and which one is for you.

Chapter Five:
How to Use Disks

Section 1:
Types of Disks

Essential information

There are three types of disk that you can use on your computer. They are:

```
CD-ROM

DVD

3½" Floppy
```

CD-ROM

If you already use a CD player then you will probably be aware that a CD-ROM is a silver-coloured plastic disk that can store an amazing amount of information. But besides carrying music, a CD can also hold a computer program, a computer game, an encyclopaedia, a supermarket shopping trolley and a whole variety of other things – the list is virtually endless.

JARGON BUSTER
CD-ROM
stands for **C**ompact **D**isk - **R**ead **O**nly **M**emory. This means that you can only read information from the disk and are unable to use it for saving your own information.

DVD
A DVD is similar to a CD in appearance. If you have a newer system, then you will probably have a separate DVD drawer. It is now possible to use DVDs to play films on your computer.

Top Tip
Hold a CD-ROM or DVD by the edges and never touch the face of the disk. Dirt and fingermarks can seriously damage the surface.

3½" Floppy
The standard 3½" floppy disk has a rigid plastic body which contains a thin flexible magnetic disk. At one end is a slider that protects the disk from dust and damage. When the disk is placed into the computer's floppy disk slot, the slider moves across to allow the machine to read or write onto the magnetic disk.

Floppy disks are a quick, cheap and easy way of storing information from your computer and for transporting information from one computer to another. However, they hold a limited amount of information and eventually become full.

Section 2:
How to Insert, Eject and Autorun a CD-ROM or DVD

Action 1
Switch on your computer and wait until your Windows application has finished loading. Identify the correct drive. If you have two drives, one will be identified as CD and the other as DVD. Press the button on the front of the drive and wait until the drawer opens out towards you.

Top Tip

Any DVD drive will also read CDs, but not vice versa. If you have a newer PC with one drawer for both CD and DVD this problem will naturally not arise.

Action 2
Place the disk in the drawer with the label upwards. Gently push the drawer back into the computer. To eject the disk, press the button adjacent to the drawer.

Action 3
Many disks will now autorun and you will begin to see the program being loaded onto the screen. Should the disk fail to autorun, look in the disk case for

information and follow the instructions included. If it still does not run, go to Section 3.

A DVD should run automatically but if you are having problems, phone the helpline on the disk packaging. (Check how much they charge per minute before you call.)

Section 3:
CD-ROM that does not Autorun

Action 1
Click once on **Start**, then click on **Run**. A dialogue box called **Run** opens (Fig. 1). Sometimes just clicking on Run alerts the computer that there is a disk in the drive and it will then autorun. If not, go to Action 2.

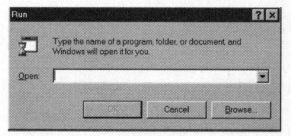

Fig. 1

Action 2

Click in the text box and try typing one of the following, then click OK (D is the letter of your CD drive).

      D:\START.EXE   D:\AUTORUN.EXE
      D:\SETUP   D:\   \START.EXE
          D:\   \SETUP.EXE

In the last two instances, type the name of the program that you are installing in the space. If none of the above have worked, try typing the same phrases one at a time, but this time in lower case.

Top Tip

To check the drive that is used for your CD, double-click on **My Computer** on the desktop and you will see the following icon: (D:)

The letter of the drive is written under the icon. If it is a letter other than D, replace D with the relevant letter (Section 3, Action 2).

Action 3

If the disk still does not run, try phoning the helpline found inside the disk packaging in the front of the CD. (Check how much they charge per minute before you call.)

Section 4:
Playing a Music CD on Computer

Essential Information
Make sure that your computer is equipped with speakers or headphones. These will plug into the back of the computer. Headphones can also be plugged directly into the CD player.

Action 1
Click once on **Start**, then **Programs**. Go to **Accessories**, then **Multimedia** and then click once on **Media Player** (Office 97, Fig. 2) or **CD Player** (Works/Office 2000, Fig. 3).

Fig. 2
Office 97

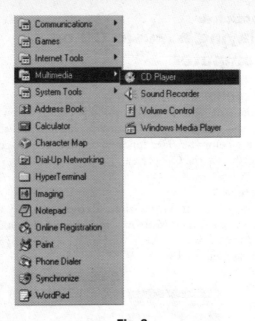

Fig. 3
Works 2000 and Office 2000

Action 2

Now go to Section 5 for Office 97 or Section 6 for
Office/Works 2000.

Section 5:
Office 97

Action 1

A new window will open called **Media Player** (Fig. 4).

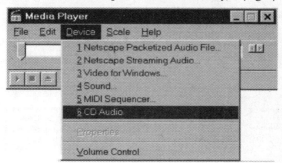

Fig. 4

Action 2

Click on **Device** on the menu bar and from the drop-down menu click on **CD Audio** (Fig. 4). The following box opens:

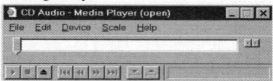

Fig. 5

Notice the operational buttons are grey and not yet activated.

Action 3

Load the CD as in Section 2. Wait a moment as the CD is engaged (you may hear a slight 'brrrr' noise) and then the buttons on the box will become black and operational. Click on the **Play** button to start the music.

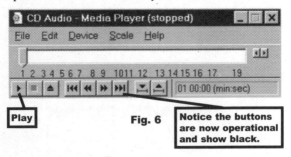

Fig. 6

Action 4

Once the music is playing, the **Play** button on Office 97 becomes the **Pause** button. The buttons from left to right are: pause, stop, eject, previous mark, rewind, fast forward, next mark, standard selection, end selection.

Fig. 7

Action 5
When you wish to close this box, click on the **Stop** button and then click on the cross in the sizing box.

Action 6
If you want to adjust the volume, **either**:
Click once on **Device** on the menu bar of the CD Player box (Fig. 4) and then click once on **Volume Control or**
Click on **Start**, **Programs**, **Accessories**, **Multimedia** and then click once on **Volume Control** (see Fig. 2).

On the Volume Control box (Fig. 8) click and drag on the Volume Control slider for CD to adjust the volume to the required level.

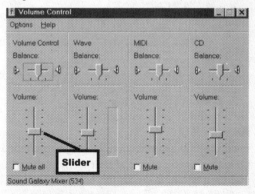

Fig. 8

Section 6:
Office 2000 and Works 2000

Action 1

A new box opens called **CD Player** (Fig. 9).

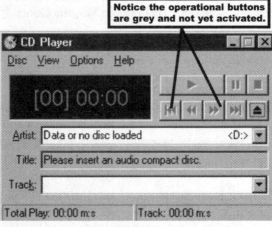

Notice the operational buttons are grey and not yet activated.

Fig. 9

Action 2

Load the CD as in Section 2. Wait a moment as the CD is engaged (you may hear a slight 'brrrr' noise) and then the buttons on the box will become black and operational.

Action 3

Click on the **Play** button to start the music (Fig. 10).

Fig. 10

Action 4

Once the music is playing, the **Pause** and **Stop** buttons become operational and show black (Fig. 11). Buttons from left to right are: play (grey), pause, stop, previous track, skip backwards, skip forwards, next track, eject.

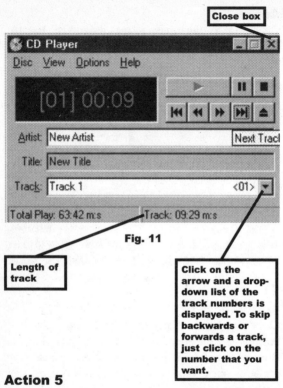

Close box

Fig. 11

Length of track

Click on the arrow and a drop-down list of the track numbers is displayed. To skip backwards or forwards a track, just click on the number that you want.

Action 5

When you wish to close this box, click on the **Stop** button and then click on either the cross in the sizing box or click on **Disc** and then on **Exit**.

Action 6

If you want to adjust the volume, either click once on
View on the menu bar of the CD Player box and then
click once on **Volume Control** (Fig. 12),

Fig. 12

or, click once on **Start**, **Programs**, **Accessories**,
Multimedia and then click once on **Volume
Control** (see Fig. 13). To adjust the volume to the
required level, click and drag on the Volume Control
slider for CD in the Volume Control box.

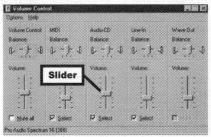

Fig. 13

Section 7:
Loading and Running Computer Games on CD

Load the CD as in Section 2. Most games will autorun. Once the game is loaded, just follow the instructions on the screen and you can start.

For more on games, see *Chapter Four: How to Play Computer Games*.

Section 8:
How to Load and Eject a 3½" Floppy

Action 1
Identify the floppy slot in your systems unit. Insert the floppy, slider first. If it does not go easily into the slot, turn it over and try the other way around.

Action 2
To eject the floppy, press the button adjacent to the disk.

Action 3
To discover how to save and open files and folders on a floppy disk, see pages 121 - 129.

Chapter Six:
How to Stay in Control of Your PC

Section 1:
The Control Panel

Essential Information
The Control Panel gives you access to many functions on your computer. It allows you to alter settings, add and remove programs and generally changes things to suit your requirements.

Action 1
There are two ways to open the Control Panel. Click on **Start** on the taskbar at the bottom of the screen. Then highlight **Settings** and move across to **Control Panel** and click once (Fig. 1).

Fig. 1

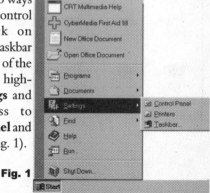

187

Alternatively, double-click on the desktop icon called **My Computer** and a new window will open. Double-click on the folder called **Control Panel** and the Control Panel window opens (Fig. 2).

Fig. 2

Section 2:
The Desktop

Essential Information

It is possible to change the background of your desktop and your screen saver whenever you feel like a change.

JARGON BUSTER
Screen Saver

An image that replaces the screen image after a period of user inactivity. If the same image is on the computer screen too long, it can 'burn' on to the screen. The screen saver will disappear as soon as you move the mouse.

Action 1
Open the Control Panel.

Action 2
Double-click on **Display** and a new box opens called **Display Properties** which has four tabs (Fig. 3). Click on the Background tab.

Action 3
Look at Figure 3. Notice the small monitor where you can see a preview of the desktop background. The two text boxes underneath called **Pattern** and **Wallpaper** list the various styles of background. 'Tile' will allow you to set the style for the whole desktop. 'Center' will set a part of the style in the centre of the screen only. Click on either.

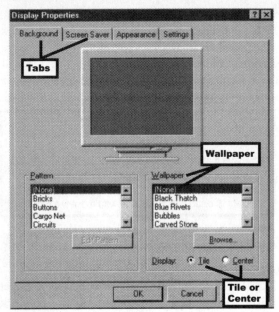

Fig. 3

Action 4

Use the scroll bars on both of these boxes to find a background that appeals to you. Click on the name and a preview will show in the small monitor. When you find one that you wish to keep, click on **Apply** and then click **OK**. Close all the open windows to return to your desktop to view your choice.

Action 5

To remove backgrounds, open up Display Properties as in Action 1. Use the scroll bars to find and highlight **[None]** on both the boxes, click **Apply** then **OK** and the background will be returned to normal. Close Display Properties and Control Panel.

Section 3:
The Screen Saver

Action 1

Open up Display Properties (if not already open) as in Section 2. Click on the Screen Saver tab (Fig. 4.)

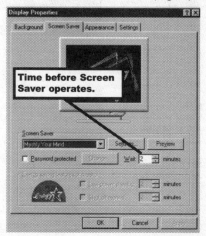

Fig. 4

Action 2

The monitor at the top of this window gives you a preview of the selection.

To change the screen saver, click once on the downward pointing arrow in the section called Screen Saver and a list of other screen saver titles will be displayed (Fig. 5).

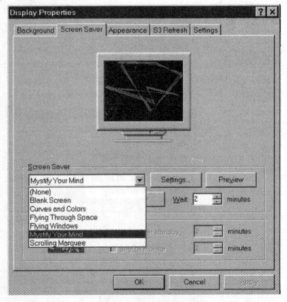

Fig. 5

Click on one that appeals and it will be previewed on the small monitor.

Action 3

The wait time before the screen saver actually operates can also be changed. In the box entitled **Wait** there are two arrows pointing up and down. Use these to increase or decrease the time before the screen saver operates.

Top Tip

It is probably a good idea to have the Screen Saver 'wait time' set for at least 3 minutes. It can become very irritating if the screen disappears every time you pause for thought!

Action 4

When you have completed your selection, click on **Apply** and then click **OK**.

Section 4:
Sounds

Essential Information
You will need speakers or headphones attached to your
computer in order to hear sounds.

Action 1
Open the
Control Panel
(Fig. 1). Double-
click on the
Sounds icon.
A new box
opens called
**Sound
Properties**
(Fig. 6).

Fig. 6

In the top half of this box you will see a list of **Events**
with little pictures of loudspeakers next to them. The
ones with loudspeakers already have sounds attached
to them. The **Name** of the sound is shown in the
next box down, along with the option of previewing
the sound.

Action 2

Highlight an Event. If it has a loudspeaker next to it the name of the sound will be in the **Sound Name** box. If it did not have a loudspeaker alongside it then **[None]** will be the Sound Name.

Click once on the downward pointing arrow in the **Sound Name** box and a number of titles of sounds are displayed with a scroll bar to view others. Click on one that appeals (Fig. 7).

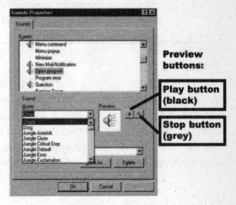

Preview buttons:

Play button (black)

Stop button (grey)

Fig. 7

Click once on the **Preview** button to see if you like the sound that you have chosen. Click on **Stop** to end the sound. Highlight another until you find one you like.

Action 3

Once you are happy with the sound, click on **Apply** at the bottom of the box, then click **OK** and the sound will play whenever that particular action is performed.

Top Tip

Sounds are great fun and can act as useful reminders. However, resist the temptation to allocate a sound to as many things as you can – they will cease to be effective as an alert.

Action 4

To remove sounds, open up **Sound Properties** as you did in Action 1. Highlight the relevant **Event**. In the **Sound Name** text box, click on the downward pointing arrow to get a drop-down list of sounds and use the scroll bars to find **[None]**. Highlight it, click on **Apply** and **OK**. The sound has now been removed.

Section 5:
The Mouse

Action 1

Open the Control Panel, double-click on the mouse icon and the Mouse Properties window will open (Fig. 8).

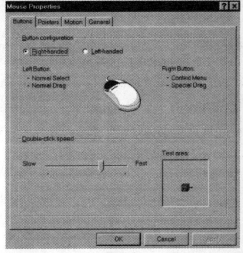

Fig. 8

Action 2

Notice that there are four tabs. Click on the **Buttons** tab. There are three parts to this tab: Button configuration, Double-click speed, and the Test area.

Action 3

The Button configuration allows you to alter the mouse button for the convenience of a right- or left-handed person. Click on the radio button for left-handed and the button colour changes. Click on the right-hand radio button and the colour reverts to original. Choose the correct button for you. Click on **Apply**, then **OK**.

Action 4

The double-clicking speed and test area are covered in *Chapter One: How to Get Started, Section 5*.

Action 5

Click on the tab marked **Pointers** (Fig. 8a).

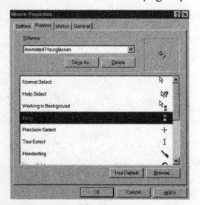

Fig. 8a

Click on the arrow by the box called **Scheme** and a drop-down menu will allow you to select different styles of pointers or cursors. When you have chosen a style, click on **Apply** and then **OK**.

Action 6

Click on the tab called **Motion** (Fig. 8b). By adjusting the sliders (using click and drag), it is possible to vary the pointer speed and trail. If you wish to experiment with the pointer trail, click the check box next to **Show pointer trail** so that it shows a tick. You can then decide whether you want to see a long trail or a short one by moving the slider between short and long. When you are happy with your choice, click on **Apply** and then **OK**.

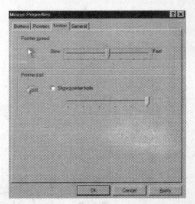

Fig. 8b

Section 6:
Date and Time

Essential Information
You may need to adjust the date and time on your computer.

Action 1
Click on the Control Panel. Click on **Date/Time**. A new window opens up called **Date/Time Properties**. This window has two tabs on it. Choose the **Date/Time** tab.

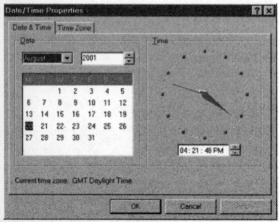

Fig. 9

It is possible to change the computer clock (notice that the time is always shown in the bottom right-hand corner of the screen), the month and the year.

Action 2

To change the time, you need to alter the digital time in the box directly beneath the clock. Click in the box and highlight a pair of numbers (hours, minutes or seconds) and use the upward and downward pointing arrows to change the numbers. The clock face will follow. Click **Apply** then **OK**.

Action 3

To the left of the clock is a calendar and above it are two boxes. One shows the month and the other the year. By clicking on the arrows to the right of the boxes you can change the month and year. Click **Apply** then **OK**.

Action 4

Close down the Control Panel and you will be returned to the desktop.

Section 7:
Keyboard Properties

Essential Information
This program allows you to dictate the pace at which
letters appear on the screen, the rate at which the
cursor blinks, and the language in which the keyboard
is set.

Action 1
Open the Control Panel. Double-click on **Keyboard**.
A new window will open called **Keyboard
Properties**. Choose the **Language** tab. You can see
from Figure 10 that the language in which the
keyboard has been set is British English.

Fig. 10

Action 2

Select the **Speed** tab (Fig. 11). Notice that this has two sections: the first is **Character repeat rate** and the second is **Cursor blink rate**. Look at the **Character repeat rate**. This speedometer dictates how fast the letters come up on the screen. Move the indicator right down to slow. Now click in the white text box and hold down a key and notice the speed at which it is repeated. Very slow! Return the indicator to a sensible speed that you find comfortable.

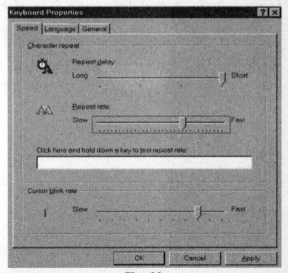

Fig. 11

Action 3

Look at the **Cursor blink rate.** Change the speed from where it is at the moment right up to fast and notice the speed of the cursor. Move the indicator back to around where it was originally.

Top Tip

Find a speed level that feels to you to be a good 'blinking' rate. There is no correct speed but it is best not to have a rate that is very slow as it may cause you to lose the cursor amongst the text!

Action 4

When you are happy with your choice of speed, click on **Apply** and then **OK.**

Section 8:
Installing and Removing Programs

Essential Information
When you install a program on your hard drive it will take up space. If this program is a game it can use up a large amount of memory. If you keep adding programs, eventually the hard disk will become full.

Top Tip

It is a good idea to remove programs as soon as they become unwanted in order to free up space.

Action 1
To load a program, place the disk into the correct slot and gently push it into the machine. If it does not start straight away, try opening the Control Panel. Double-click on **Add/Remove Programs**. A new box opens called **Add/Remove Program Properties**. Click on the **Install/Uninstall** tab (Fig. 12). Click once on the **Install** button and let the computer find the drive and install the program.

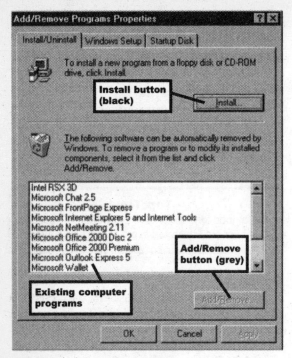

Fig. 12

Action 2

Click on Start on the taskbar and then click on **Run** to tell the computer that a disk has been inserted (Fig. 13).

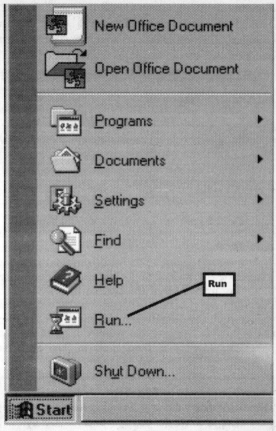

Fig. 13

Action 3

If the CD still does not start loading, have a look at the CD's packaging. This should tell you what to type into the text box of the Run window to get the CD loading (Fig. 14).

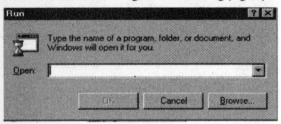

Fig. 14

If all else fails, phone the manufacturer's helpline.

Action 4

To remove a Program, open **Add/Remove Program Properties** as in Action 1. The existing computer programs are shown in the bottom half of the box. Highlight the program that you want to delete and click once on the **Add/Remove** button. The computer will ask if you are sure that you wish to delete this program. If you are, then click on 'Yes' and the computer will remove the program.

Top Tip

Beware. Once the computer has deleted a program there is no way of getting it back, except by reinstalling the program from floppy disk or CD.

Section 9:
Adding New Hardware

Essential Information
You may want to add a new piece of equipment, like a printer, to your computer set-up. The computer has to be told that there is an addition. Once it has been told about the new hardware it then has to search through all its systems to find it, key into it and make it operational.

Action 1
Open the Control Panel. Double-click on the **Add New Hardware** icon. A new window appears called **Add New Hardware Wizard**. Read the instructions that it gives.

Note the three buttons at the bottom:

> **<Back, Next>** and **Cancel**.

Action 2
Click **Next>**. The Wizard asks you, 'Do you want Windows to search for your new hardware?' Click the 'Yes' radio button. Click **Next>**.

Action 3

The Wizard now warns you of three things:
1. To *close all open programs*. You must close down other programs that you are working on.
2. That a *progress indicator* will appear whilst detection is in progress.
3. That if the indicator stops for a long while *you may need to restart* the computer.
Click **Next>**.

Action 4

The Wizard now tells you that it will look for the new hardware. It also gives you a warning. Read it! Note the blue broken strip at the bottom of the window: the detection progress indicator. You will now have to wait until the detection process is completed. The screen may go black but it will gradually come back to normal.

Action 5

Eventually the Wizard will say that it has finished detecting hardware. If it has not found anything it will ask if you wish to install a specific device manually.

Action 6

To do this, highlight the hardware type and click **Next>**. You will now be guided by the Wizard through a series of instructions. Read and follow them carefully.

Section 10:
Find

Essential Information

Find is a very useful tool in helping you to trawl through the computer memory to find lost files. We all make mistakes. It is very easy to save a file in the wrong place accidentally. You may have intended to save a file or folder on a floppy disk but because your attention was momentarily distracted, it has ended up being saved somewhere else. The problem is, where? Another common problem is forgetting the exact name of the file as well as its location.

Top Tip

It's a good idea to discover how to use Find before it is actually needed. A mistake then becomes just irritating rather than a disaster.

Action 1

To locate **Find**, click on the **Start** button and then move the pointer up the menu and allow it to rest on **Find**. Another menu will be displayed (Fig. 15).

Click on **Files and Folders** and the **Find: All Files** box is opened (Fig. 16). Click on the **Name and Location** tab.

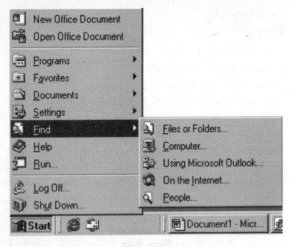

Fig. 15

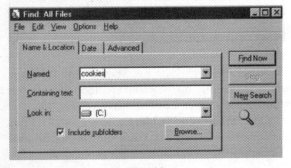

Fig. 16

Action 2

In the **Named:** text box type in the name (or as close to the name as possible) of the file or folder that you are searching for. In Figure 16 a search is being made for a word document called Cookies. Click on the arrow of the drop-down list box called **Look in** and select the area of the computer that you wish to search. Figure 16 shows a search in C, which is the hard drive (sometimes called the hard disk).

Click on **Find Now.** The computer will now search its memory and while this is going on the little magnifying glass will rotate.

Action 3

Eventually the computer will finish searching and present you with a list of files and folders with names or similar names to the one that you typed into the text box.

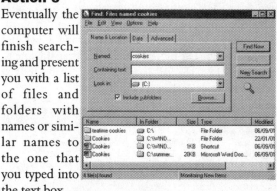

Fig. 17

213

Action 4

With luck the list will include the file for which you are searching. In Figure 17 you can see four items that responded to the search for Cookies. Notice that details are given of when the items were last modified (worked on) – this will give you a clue as to which might be the correct item. The list also tells you what type of files they are and where the file or folder has been saved.

Action 5

Sometimes you may need to expand the heading called **In Folder** in order to read all the words. To do this, simply place the pointer on the line between **In Folder** and **Size**. The pointer will change to a black cross with two arrowheads. This will allow you to resize the headings in the direction of the arrows. Click and hold down the left mouse button and drag the line to the right (Fig. 18). All the headings can be resized (made wider or narrower) in this way.

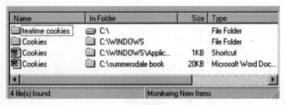

Fig. 18

You can now see that the Word document, Cookies, has been saved in a folder called Summersdale Book on C (the hard drive).

Action 6
In order to open the document, double-click on the entry listed.

Section 11:
Creating Shortcuts

It is very easy to create shortcuts to the programs and files which you frequently use. The shortcut will be in the form of an icon that will sit on your desktop. By moving the pointer onto the icon and double-clicking, you will be taken straight into the program or file without having to navigate the usual pathway.

You can create shortcuts from a number of the Microsoft Windows and it is the same procedure for all of them. Here are three examples.

Windows Explorer
Open Windows Explorer (Start, Programs). On the right side of Windows Explorer, highlight the file or folder that requires a shortcut. In Figure 19, for example, 'teatime cookies' is shown as highlighted.

Click on **File** and then click on **Create Shortcut** on the drop-down menu. A new icon will appear on the right side entitled **Shortcut to...** and then the name of the folder. In Figure 20 for example, there is now a shortcut called **Shortcut to teatime cookies**.

Explorer window and onto the desktop. If not enough

of the desktop is visible for you to do this, click on the title bar of the window and drag it to one side, revealing more desktop. (For more on Windows Explorer see *Chapter Seven: How to Create and Manage Files*.) Close Windows Explorer.

My Computer

Alternatively, open My Computer (double-click on the icon on the desktop). Highlight the file or folder for which you wish to create a shortcut. Click on File and select **Create Shortcut** from the drop-down menu. In Figure 21 for example, the Control Panel has been selected.

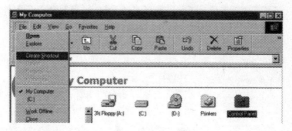

Depending on the program that you have selected, the following box may appear:

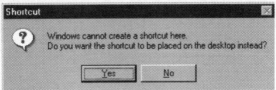

if you click on "Yes" the shortcut will be placed directly onto the desktop and you will not need to click and drag it across.

Control Panel

The Control Panel is another window where shortcuts can be created. The procedure is exactly the same as in the previous examples.

Removing Shortcuts

Action 1
Make sure that you are looking at the desktop.

Action 2
Click once on the shortcut to be deleted and it will change colour. Click on the *right* mouse button and a drop-down menu will appear (Fig. 24). Highlight the word 'Delete' and press Return. A **Confirm File Delete** box will appear on the screen (Fig. 25).

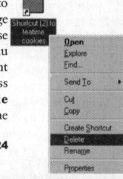

Fig. 24

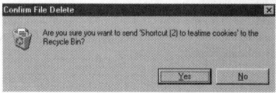

Select 'Yes' and the shortcut will be removed from the desktop. It is only the shortcut icon on the desktop that has been deleted, not the actual program or file, which can still be reached in the usual way.

Section 13:

The Taskbar and Start Menu

Essential Information

The Start button, which sits on the taskbar, provides the pathway into your PC and its programs. The taskbar is the grey strip that runs along the bottom of the screen, and programs that are currently running appear on it as buttons (Fig. 26). This allows you to see at a glance which programs are open and to recall them to the screen by clicking on the relevant program button on the taskbar.

Although the taskbar usually sits along the bottom of the screen, it can be accidentally moved to any of the four sides of the screen. Should this occur, simply place the pointer on a clear part of the grey strip and then click and drag it back to its usual position. It is possible to make alterations to the Start menu and the taskbar. To do this you need to open the Taskbar Properties box.

Action 1

Click on the **Start** button, move up the menu and select **Settings**, move across and highlight **Taskbar and Start Menu**. Click once.

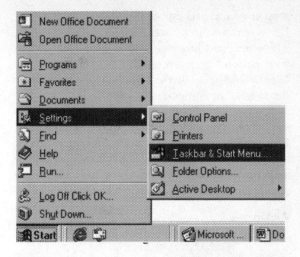

Action 2

A box opens called **Taskbar Properties** with two tabs. Click on the tab called **Taskbar Options** (Fig. 27).

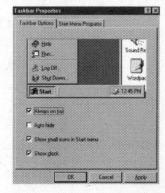

Fig. 27

This shows a small

221

section of the desktop, including the Start menu. Below are four check boxes, each set against an option. These options allow you to alter some items to suit your personal preferences. You can choose to have large or small icons on the Start menu for example, or not to have the computer clock visible.

You can also customise the actual taskbar. To read more about changes to the taskbar use the **What's This?** help (see *Chapter Three: How to Use Microsoft Help*).

If you decide to change options, make sure a tick is added or removed from the check box. Then click **Apply** and **OK.**

Action 3

Select the tab called **Start Menu Programs** (Fig. 28).

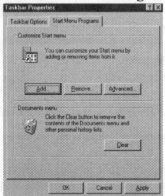

Fig. 28

This box is in two sections. The top section allows you to add or remove programs to the Start menu but it is probably a good idea to wait until you are more experienced before attempting to do this. Beneath it is the section called **Documents Menu**. As you create documents, they will be listed for your convenience on the Documents menu, which can be accessed from the Start menu (see Fig. 29).

Fig. 29

These act as shortcuts, because by clicking on a document name it will open directly onto the screen. However, after a while the list can become very long and it may be a good idea to clear it. To do this, click on the **Clear** button, then click **OK** and the Documents menu will be cleared.

Chapter Seven:
How to Create and Manage Files

Essential Information

It is essential to manage files and folders on your PC and the most popular way of doing this is through Windows Explorer.

Windows Explorer allows you to view the contents of disks and folders on hard and floppy disks and to create your own folders. This facility will enable you to organise and manage information and work more effectively. This in turn will allow you to feel in control of your computer.

Section 1:
Finding Windows Explorer

Action 1

Open Windows Explorer by following the path shown in Figure 1.

Fig. 1
Path to Windows Explorer

Highlight Windows Explorer and click once. Windows
Explorer opens.

Action 2

Click on **View** on the menu bar of Windows Explorer. On the drop-down menu, follow the path to **Explorer Bar** and make sure there is a tick by the side of Folders.

Action 3

Windows Explorer is now divided into two parts with the Folders bar on the left and the contents on the right. Look at the left pane. Identify on your screen the following: Desktop, My Computer, Recycle Bin.

Fig. 2

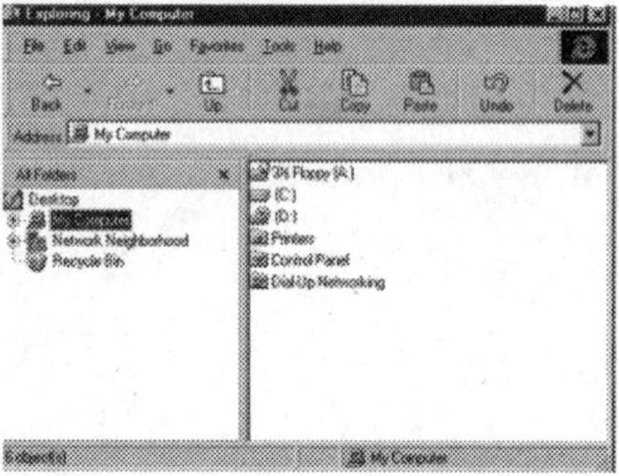

Action 4

Move the pointer onto the Desktop and click once. The contents of the Desktop will be displayed in the right half of Explorer.

Click on My Computer. The contents will be displayed on the right pane. Do the same to Recycle Bin. When a folder is highlighted on the left, its contents are displayed on the right.

Section 2:
Looking at Folders

Essential Information
Notice folders or icons with a plus sign alongside them. This indicates that the folder or icon contains further objects. A folder with a minus sign means that it is already open. The contents will be listed below the folder on the left side of Windows Explorer.

Action 1
Move the pointer to the plus sign next to My Computer and click once. The folder opens out and more folders are listed (Fig. 3). By the side of My Computer is a minus sign showing that the folder is open.

Fig. 3

227

Action 2

Fig. 4

Look on the left side of Explorer and find Hard Disk (C:). Move the pointer onto the Hard Disk (C:), and click once. Hard Disk (C:) is highlighted and on the right side of Explorer are displayed the folders contained on Hard Disk (C:).

Move the pointer onto the plus sign by Hard Disk (C:) in the left side of Windows Explorer, click once and the folder opens. The folders and single files held on the Hard Disk (C:) are displayed on the left of Explorer (Fig. 4).

Notice that single files are not displayed on the left, only on the right (Fig. 4).

Action 3

Move the pointer back onto the left pane. Close the Hard Disk (C:) folder by clicking on the minus sign by the side of Hard Disk (C:). The contents are returned to the Hard Disk folder.

Action 4

Insert a floppy disk. Move the pointer onto the left side of Explorer and onto 3½ Floppy (A:), and click once. 3½ Floppy (A:) is highlighted and the contents are displayed on the right of Explorer.

Now move the pointer back onto the minus sign by My Computer, click once and the contents are returned to the folder. The minus symbol is replaced by a plus sign.

Section 3:
Viewing and Arranging Icons

It is possible to choose to have large or small icons on Windows Explorer and to arrange them in various ways. To do this, go to **View** and select either **Large** or **Small Icons** (Figs. 5 and 6). To arrange icons, go to **View** and select **Arrange Icons**. Figure 7 shows the drop-down menu from which you should click on your personal preference.

Fig. 5
Small Icons

Viewing and Arranging Icons

Fig. 6
Large Icons

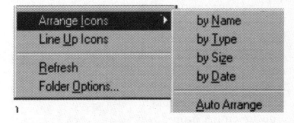

Fig. 7
Arrange Icons menu

Section 4:
Creating your own Folders

Essential Information
Windows Explorer can also be used to create, delete and move folders. Use these folders to house documents or files that you produce and to remove unwanted items when they have served their purpose. This function can be used on the hard drive as well as on a floppy disk.

Action 1
Move the pointer to the plus sign next to My Computer and click once. The folder opens out. Look on the left and find Hard Disk (C:) once again. Click on it once so that it is highlighted.

Move your cursor so that it is on the right side of Windows Explorer and on a blank white section free of any files or folders. Click once on the right mouse button, making sure that you do not accidentally highlight a document. A drop-down menu appears (Fig. 8).

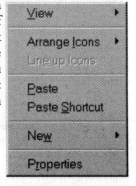

Fig. 8
Drop-down menu resulting from right mouse click

If a different menu has appeared then you have probably clicked on the left side of Windows Explorer or highlighted a document on the right pane. To rectify this, move the pointer onto an empty white section on the right side of Explorer and click once on the right mouse button. The drop-down menu should then appear.

Action 2

On the drop-down menu, move the pointer onto the word 'New' but do not click. Wait a moment and another drop-down menu will appear (Fig. 9).

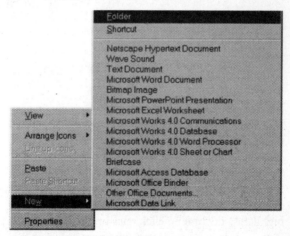

Fig. 9

Move the pointer onto this menu and click once on the word 'Folder'. A new yellow folder will appear on the right side of Windows Explorer. It will be placed at the end of the list of folders and files and will be labelled 'New Folder' (Fig. 10).

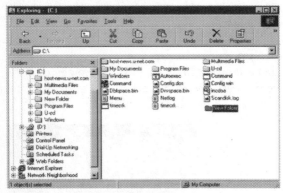

Fig. 10

Action 3

The same procedure can be used to create folders on a floppy disk. Insert a disk and on the left side of Explorer, click on 3½ Floppy (A:), so that it is highlighted.

Move your cursor so that it is on the right side of Windows Explorer, on a blank section free of any files or folders. Making sure that you do not accidentally highlight a document, click once on the right mouse button. A drop-down menu appears as in Figure 8.

On the drop-down menu, move the pointer on to the word 'New' but do not click. Wait a moment and another drop-down menu will appear (Fig. 9). Move the pointer across onto the menu and click once on the word 'Folder'. A new yellow folder labelled 'New Folder' will have appeared on the right side of Windows Explorer at the end of the list of folders and files.

Section 5:
Naming a Folder

The process for naming a folder is the same for hard and floppy disks.

Action 1
To give a folder a name, place the pointer onto the new folder and click once on the *left* mouse button. This will highlight the folder and also cause the text cursor to pulse in the 'New Folder' box.

Action 2
Delete the words 'New Folder' and type in the name of your choice for the folder. Move the pointer onto a blank section of Windows Explorer and click once. The new folder will now have turned yellow like the other folders in the list and its name will be set. The folder can now be used to store files and documents or even other folders that you create. See Section 7 on how to move files into folders.

Section 6:
Renaming a Folder

The process for renaming a folder is the same for hard and floppy disks.

Action 1
Place the pointer onto the folder to be renamed. Click once on the right mouse button and a drop-down menu appears (Fig. 11).

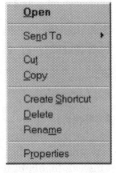

Fig. 11

Action 2
Left-click on the word 'Rename'. The menu will then disappear and the text cursor will be present in the folder box. Press the **Delete** key to remove the old file name and then type the new name that you have chosen.

Action 3
Move the pointer onto a blank part of Windows Explorer, click once on the left mouse button and the new name is set.

Section 7:
Placing Files in a Folder

The process of placing a file in a folder is the same for hard and floppy disks.

Action 1
Open Windows Explorer. On the left side of Explorer, locate the folder that you are going to use for housing your files. The files will also be listed on the left side of Windows Explorer.

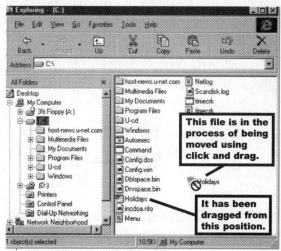

Fig. 12

237

Action 2

Locate the file on the right-hand side that you wish to place in the folder. Place the pointer on the file, click and hold down the left mouse button and you will be able to move the file (click and drag). As long as you keep the left mouse button depressed you will be able to move the file. While the file is on the right side of Explorer it will look like Figure 12.

Action 3

Drag the file onto the left side of Explorer. As it moves into this section it acquires an arrow (Fig. 13).

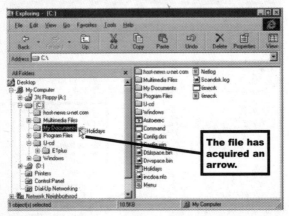

Fig. 13

Carefully place the arrow over the selected folder. The selected folder will also become highlighted in blue. Release the left mouse button, moving the file into the folder.

Action 4

To check that it has worked, click on the folder that has just received the file on the left side of Windows Explorer. The folder will open and the file should now be listed on the right side of Windows Explorer.

Section 8:
Lost Files

Don't panic if you think you have lost your file whilst trying to move it. Click on the Hard Disk (C:) or 3½ Floppy Disk (A:) (whichever you are using) on the left side of Windows Explorer and check to see whether the document is still listed on the right side of Explorer as a single document (still outside the folder). If it is, try moving it into the folder again.

If you still cannot see the file then you may have placed it accidentally into another folder. Don't worry, it will not harm any of the other folders or programs. Try opening up any of the folders which were in the immediate proximity of the correct folder.

If you still cannot find it then it is worth asking the computer to find the file for you. Read *Chapter Six: How to Stay in Control of Your PC*, page 211 on finding files.

Section 9:
Deleting and Removing Folders

Essential Information

Using Windows Explorer it is possible to remove and delete files and folders from the hard disk (C:) and floppy disk (A:).

Action 1

Open up Windows Explorer. On the left side of Explorer select Hard Disk (C:). You may need to open the My Computer folder first.

Action 2

Once Hard Disk (C:) is highlighted in blue, look on the right of Explorer. The files and folders contained on the hard disk will be listed. Click once on the file or folder that you wish to remove.

Action 3

Now go to **File** on the menu bar, click once and a drop-down menu appears. Find **Delete** and click once (Fig. 14).

Fig. 14

A window called **Confirm File Delete** appears (Fig. 15).

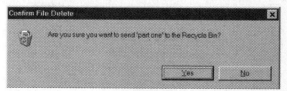

Fig. 15

If you have made a mistake and you decide that you wish to retain the item after all, you can click on 'No' and the delete will be cancelled.

If you click on 'Yes', the file or folder will be removed from the hard disk and sent to the Recycle Bin.

Section 10:
Deleting Files or Folders from a Floppy Disk

Essential Information
This is a similar process to deleting items from the hard disk but once a file is deleted from a floppy disk it is lost forever – it does not go to the Recycle Bin.

Action 1
Open Windows Explorer and highlight 3½ Floppy (A:) on the left of the window. Files and folders contained on the floppy become listed on the right half of Explorer. Highlight the item that you wish to delete, go to File on the menu bar and click on **Delete**.

A **Confirm File Delete** window appears (Fig. 16).

Fig. 16

Be certain at this stage that you really wish to remove an item because once deleted it cannot be recalled. It is irrevocably erased. If you wish to keep the document, click on 'No'.

Action 2
If you are still certain that you wish to delete the item, click on 'Yes' in the Confirm Delete File window and the item will be erased from the floppy disk.

Section 11:
The Recycle Bin

Essential Information
Look at Figure 2 and notice the Recycle Bin in the left side of Windows Explorer. When a file has been deleted from your hard disk it is automatically placed in the Recycle Bin which then acts as a receptacle for unwanted material. It is possible to restore material from the Recycle Bin back into the hard disk – useful if you have made a mistake in deleting an item! It is worthwhile creating a page specifically to be deleted in order to practise using the Recycle Bin.

Action 1
Double-click on the Recycle Bin icon on the left side of Windows Explorer. The bin's contents will be displayed on the right pane. If the bin is empty then obviously you have not yet deleted any files. If you have deleted a file from the hard disk then it will be listed here.

Action 2
To restore an item from the Recycle Bin back to its original place on the hard disk, click once on the folder or file concerned so that it is highlighted. Now click on **File** on the menu bar, then click on **Restore** on the drop-down menu (Fig. 17).

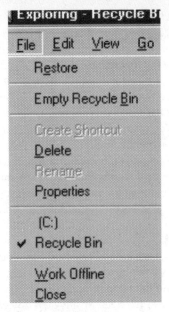

Fig. 17

The file will be returned to its original place from where it was deleted. The word 'Restore' will only appear on the menu if you actually have something to restore.

Action 3

To empty selected files or folders from the bin, click on the item concerned, then on **File**, and then click **Delete** on the drop-down menu. A message box will ask you if you are sure that you wish to delete the item. Make your decision and click on 'Yes' or 'No'.

Action 4

If you maintain a tidy hard disk and regularly get rid of unwanted or unnecessary material you will eventually find that the Recycle Bin starts to look rather full. To empty the whole bin, click on **File** and then click on **Empty Recycle Bin**. A message box called **Confirm Multiple File Delete** will ask you if you are sure that you want to delete all the items. Make your decision and then click on 'Yes' or 'No'.

Section 12:
Exploring Windows Explorer Using Help

Essential Information

Now that you have encountered Windows Explorer you may like to extend your knowledge. The Help function on the menu bar will enable you to discover more about Explorer (see *Chapter Three: How to Use Help*).

Chapter Eight:
How to Get Connected to the Internet

Section 1:
The Internet Explained

Essential Information

Put very simply, the Internet is a worldwide system of various interconnected computer networks which are linked via the telephone system and are thus able to share and exchange information.

The Internet is used for the following:

1. To host the **World Wide Web**
(see *Chapter Nine: How to Use the World Wide Web*)
2. To send and receive **e-mails**
(see *Chapter Ten: How to Use E-mail*)
3. To play **games**
4. To access **newsgroups**
5. To download **software** for your PC

Essential Requirements

1. A computer (Section 2)
2. A modem (Section 4)
3. An Internet Access and/or Service Provider (Section 9)

Section 2:
What sort of computer do I need to access the Internet?

New Computer

If you are purchasing a new set-up, try to buy a computer that has a fast processor and a large memory. This is more important than buying a package with lots of useless software that you will never use. The speed of a processor is measured in MHz or GHz. Aim for the highest number of MHz or GHz that you can afford. MB RAM is used to describe the size of computer memory. Try to get a computer with at least 128 MB RAM. The larger the memory, the faster the computer is able to work and to download material from the Internet.

JARGON BUSTER

MHz = Megahertz
GHz = Gigahertz

These are the units of speed at which the processor works. The higher the number, the faster the processor.

1,000 MHz = 1 GHz.

Existing Computer

If you have an existing computer that is slower and with a smaller memory, then don't despair. You can still get onto the Internet as long as you have a CD-ROM drive, at least 8 MB RAM, and are running at least Windows 3.1 or Windows 95. Your computer will not be as fast as the latest ones and you may not be able to access some of the features that the Internet offers such as games or video links, but most of the online facilities will be available to you.

Top Tip

If you find that your computer handles the Internet quite slowly, it may be a good idea to use it mainly at weekends and evenings in order to keep the telephone costs to a minimum.

JARGON BUSTER

MB = Megabyte
(a million 'bytes', or units of storage space)

GB = Gigabyte
(a thousand million bytes)

RAM = Random Access Memory,
the main memory of a computer.

Section 3:
Connecting to the Internet – Options

New Computer

If you have purchased a new set-up you may have the modem and Internet software already installed. All you need to do is plug the telephone cable into the wall socket (and plug in and turn on the computer, of course!). Now go to Section 15.

Existing Computer

1. If you have an older system and you feel unable to get your computer set up and connected to the Internet, then it may be a good idea to call in a computer engineer to do the whole thing for you (but get a quote first). Alternatively, take your computer along to a dealer and ask them to do it for you (get a quote first).

2. If you want to do as millions have done before you and do the whole thing yourself then start by reading about modems.

Section 4:
Modems

Essential Information

A modem is a device that allows your computer to connect with the telephone system. There are two types: internal or external.

The *internal* modem is mounted on a circuit board inside the central processing unit (the 'brain' of the computer). The *external* modem is housed in a small box that sits next to your computer system. If you are unsure whether your computer already has a modem installed it is very easy to check. Follow the steps below.

Action 1

Click once on **Start**, move up the menu bar to **Settings**, and then move across to the **Control Panel**, highlight and click once. The **Control Panel** window opens (Fig. 1). Double-click on the modem icon.

A new box will appear called **Modems Properties**. If you have a modem already installed the box will look like Figure 3. If you do not have a modem it will look like Figure 2.

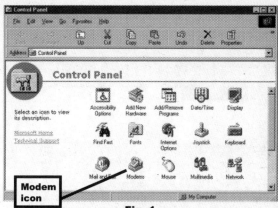

Fig. 1
Control Panel window

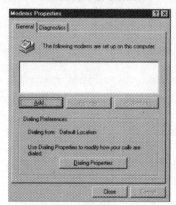

Fig. 2

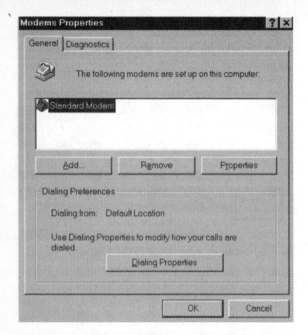

Fig. 3

Action 2

If you do not have a modem, go on to Section 5. If you already have a modem installed then go on to Section 8.

Section 5:
Installing a Modem

Essential Information
It is possible to install an external modem yourself, as it is just a case of plugging in connections. However, this can appear daunting to a beginner. If you have any doubts about your ability it may be a good idea to ask for advice or visual instructions at one of the many large computer stores. Failing this, ask a qualified computer engineer to fit it for you. If you do decide upon an external modem, aim for the fastest that you can afford and one with volume control.

Internal Modem
If you decide upon an internal modem this does need to be installed by an expert so ask a qualified engineer to do it for you. Purchase the fastest modem that you can afford.

Once your modem has been installed it will need to be detected by the computer. Go to Section 6.

Section 6:
Detecting a Modem

Essential information

The computer needs to search for this new piece of equipment (hardware) which has just been installed. There are two ways of doing this. You can either request the system to search for the modem automatically or do it manually.

Top Tip

It is a good idea to try to do a manual search for the modem as it is a way of discovering more about how the computer works. Should the system fail to automatically detect the modem you will have to use the manual system anyway!

Action 1

Click once on **Start**, move up the menu to **Settings** and then across to **Control Panel**. Double-click on the modems icon and **Modems Properties** will open (Fig. 2). Single-click on the **Add** button and the **Install a New Modem** box will appear (Fig. 4).

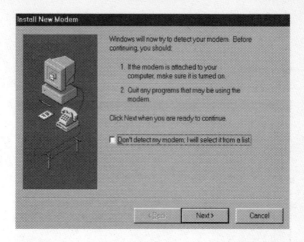

Fig. 4
Install New Modem box

Action 2

Remove the tick from the check box 'Don't detect my modem, I will select it from a list'. When you remove this tick you will automatically be leaving the computer to detect the modem. Click on **Next>** and the system will commence searching. When the search is completed a box will appear telling you whether or not the modem has been detected. If it has not then go to Action 3 for a manual search.

Action 3

Follow the procedure in Action 1 to recall Install New Modems. This time make sure that you leave the tick in the check box 'Don't detect my modem I will select it from a list'.

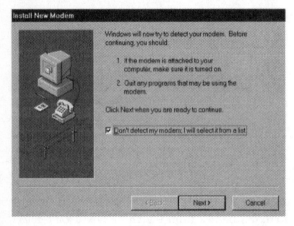

Fig. 5
Install Modem box showing the check box ticked

Action 4

Click on **Next >**. The box in Figure 6 will now ask you to select the model and make of your modem. By clicking on the arrows of the scroll bars, search both lists until you find the appropriate model and manufacturer and then highlight both. Click on **Next >** and then read the following box about communication ports.

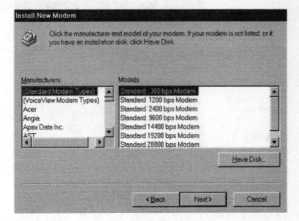

Fig. 6
Select a make and model

Section 7:
Communication Ports

Essential Information

The next box will ask you to select a communication port (Fig. 7). A communication port is a way of getting information in and out of your computer. It can be an external socket or a slot inside the systems unit.

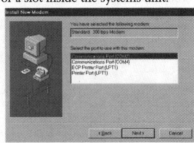

Fig. 7
Selecting a
COM Port

Action 1

If you do not already know which COM Port to select then try COM Port 2 (COM 1 is a port often used for the mouse). If a port is already being used by something else the computer will tell you that there is a conflict. If this is the case, try one of the other ports – there are four altogether.

Action 2

Once the COM Port has been selected, click on **Next >**. The system will then complete its task. When the next box appears, click on **Finish**.

Section 8:
Dialling

Essential Information

You now need to enter information about your country and telephone codes.

Action 1

To do this you need to get back to Modems Properties. If you have forgotten how to do this, follow the procedure in Section 4, Action 1.

Action 2

There are two tabs at the top called **General** and **Diagnostics**. Click once on the **General** tab, then click once on **Dialling Properties** as seen in Figures 2 and 3. The box called **Dialling Properties** will appear (Fig. 8).

Action 3

You will now need to select your country from the drop-down list and type in your area code.

If you use a call waiting facility it is a good idea to disable it. An incoming call can interrupt an Internet session. Select a number from the drop-down menu. If you are unsure, check with the phone company or a local dealer. When you have finished filling in the message box, click on **OK**.

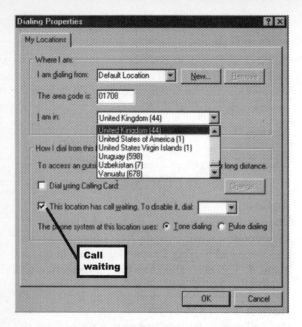

Fig. 8
Dialling Properties box

Section 9:
Internet Access and Service Providers

Essential Information

Once you have ascertained whether your computer is equipped with enough memory to deal with the Internet and you have a modem installed and detected you are almost home and dry! All you need to do now is to decide which company you are going to use to provide you with your Internet services. There are so many to choose from that it can seem daunting at first but do not be discouraged. Take your time and read on about providers.

What is an Internet Access or Service Provider?

An Internet Access Provider (or IAP) is a company that offers access to the Internet and perhaps a few other services. An Internet Service Provider (ISP) offers access to the Internet and a fuller and wider range of services than an IAP.

What is a POP (Post Office Protocol) Account?

POP accounts are local area telephone numbers that your ISP works through, enabling you to e-mail and connect to the Web at local telephone rates.

Top Tip

Aim for a server that offers you a POP 3 account because this will also enable you to access your e-mail from a variety of sources and not just via your ISP. This will give you the flexibility to read your e-mail at work, home, the library or wherever you have access to a computer.

Action 1

Look at the following and decide which aspects of the Internet you are interested in using:

- Just e-mail.
- E-mail and the World Wide Web.
- Creating and uploading your own web page/site onto the Internet.
- Online shopping.
- To play games and download software for your PC.
- To access chat/newsgroups.
- Mainly recreation or business?
- Do you wish to pay monthly/yearly for your subscription or do you want a free ISP/IAP?
- Do you want a family orientated ISP/IAP which has a restricted access facility for children?

Section 10:
Choosing an IAP/ISP

Essential Information

There are many companies today offering Internet access and a range of services and costs. The most important thing is to take your time, make enquires of each and decide whether what they are offering is actually what you want. As a beginner it is always advisable to keep things as simple as possible. Decide exactly what it is that you want from the Internet. You can then make sure that the company you choose will be delivering the services that you want and at the price that you can afford.

Below are some companies that can provide access. The list is not exclusive and does not represent any recommendation.

Some major companies currently in the market:

BT Internet Services:	0800 800001
Demon Internet:	0181 371 1234
Net Direct:	0800 731 3311
Talk 101:	01925 245145
Easynet:	0207 900 4444

Online Servers:

America Online (AOL):	0800 279 1234
CompuServe:	0800 289 378
Virgin Net:	0500 558800
Yahoo! Online:	0207 808 4400
Microsoft Network (MSN):	08457 002000
Tesco Online:	0345 225533

Companies for special groups

Some Internet Service Providers aim their services at specific groups, such as NHS People, which is an ISP for NHS staff members. There are ISPs for various regions of the UK like IofM, which is an ISP for the Isle of Man. Then there are IAP/ISPs for different religions, banks, supermarkets: the list is endless. There are directories on the Web which list all the different IAP/ISPs currently available. It might be a good idea to go on the Internet in your local library or Internet café and look at which companies are pertinent to your interests.

Here are a few examples:

Internet UK (a UK and Irish Internet company): http://www.limitless.co.uk/inetuk/

ISP Review
(offers news review and a directory of UK ISPs): http://www.ispreview.co.uk/

Herbison Consulting Gateway
(offers a worldwide gateway to ISPs):
http://www.herbison.com

The Internet Magazine:
http://www.internet-magazine.com

Directories of companies that offer free access

There are also directories of companies that offer free access to the Internet. This really is worth a trip to the library or Internet café. Look at the two directories below and print off copies of the companies that interest you. Then ring them up and find out exactly what is free and what extras you have to pay for.

Free Internet Access Directory (a directory of free access providers in the UK from Internet UK):
http://www.limitless.co.uk/inetuk/free-access.html

Net 4 Nowt:
http://www.net4nowt.com

Easy as 1-2-Free:
http://www.12free.co.uk

Section 11:
UK Libraries and Internet Cafés

The Internet is currently being installed in all UK libraries. Access is for all and is not limited to special groups such as students. There will probably be a small charge. There should be help available from library staff.

Internet or cyber cafés are also a good way of gaining an introduction to the Internet. There is usually a set charge and you only pay for the amount of time spent online and any drinks or snacks you buy. You can explore the Web or send e-mails and there is usually someone available if you get stuck. Some of the larger Internet cafés now offer short courses for beginners.

Section 12:
Contacting an IAP/ISP

Essential Information

Once you have decided what you want from an IAP/ISP and chosen a few likely companies, you may want to phone them up and discuss their services. Here are a few tips:

1. Ask for an information pack.
2. Look for a company that provides you with a CD-ROM that is preconfigured for easy installation.
3. Make sure the company that you choose uses the POP 3 mail system.
4. Do they provide a telephone helpline and what times are they available? Some work 24 hours and others only Monday to Friday and not at the weekend. Make sure a helpline is available for when you are going to be using the Internet.
5. If the helpline isn't free, how much do they charge? A charge of 50p per minute, for example, can soon mount up if you require a lot of support.
6. What is their yearly fee or monthly subscription?
7. Do not purchase an ISP/IAP that also charges you to go online. The most you should pay is your normal telephone rate.
8. What other services do they offer? Do you want them? Don't buy an ISP/IAP with bells and whistles on if all you want to do is send an e-mail.

Section 13:
Telephone Charges

Essential Information

Remember that the only way that you can connect to the Internet to send e-mails or surf the Web is to use the telephone system. Every time you go online your computer modem is making a phone call and you are paying for it.

1. Make sure your ISP only uses local phone numbers (POP 3).

2. Time how long you spend on the Internet.

3. Work offline whenever the opportunity allows.

4. Don't go online during peak periods if you can avoid it.

5. Send your ISP phone number to any of the discount schemes offered by your phone company.

Section 14:
Signing Up

Essential Information
Once you have decided upon an ISP they will send
you the necessary software on a CD-ROM.

Action 1
Every service provider will have different
instructions, but first of all you will need to load the
CD-ROM.

Action 2
You will need a password and a username. Take some
time to think of an unusual word – don't just spell
your name backwards! This password should be kept
secret. It is your security against other people using
your ISP and your phone or even accessing your
information.

Action 3
Before you begin the set-up procedure, have the
following ready:

1. The reference number on the software package.

2. If you haven't signed up and paid already by post,

you will need to do so on online, so have your credit or debit card ready.

3. The ISP will give you a username and password in order to commence, but once you are online, change these to your selection.

Action 4

A series of instructions will appear on the screen – just follow them and your set-up will be completed automatically. Remember, if you have problems, this is where that helpline is really invaluable. If you get stuck, phone.

Top Tip

If you make a mistake whilst trying to set up, don't worry, just cancel or exit the procedure and start again.

Section 15:
Connecting

Once your ISP program has been loaded onto your system, all the hard work has been completed. In future, it will be a simple process to get online.

At the end of the procedure you will have the choice of going online immediately or later.

Action 1
Open your Internet program by either double-clicking on an icon that was automatically created and placed on your desktop, or by clicking on **Start**, **Programs** and double-clicking on the ISP program listed.

A connection box will eventually appear on the screen (Fig. 9 and 9a).

Fig. 9

Fig. 9a

Enter your password,
click once on **Connect**
and your modem will
dial up your IAP/ISP.
Another box will appear
(Fig. 10 and 10a).

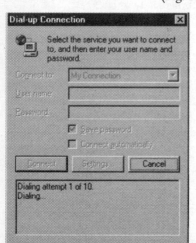

Fig. 10

Fig. 10a

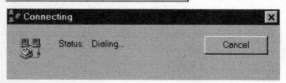

As your program connects to the ISP/IAP, a further
box will inform you that your username and password
are being checked (Fig. 11 and 11a).

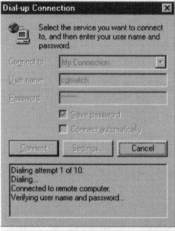

Fig. 11

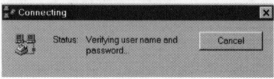

Fig.11a

If you have typed in your password correctly you will
be connected and information will begin to appear on
the monitor.

Action 2

If you have made a mistake, the following box will appear (Fig. 12 and 12a).

Fig. 12

Follow the advice in the box. You may have made a mistake when typing your password.

Fig.12a

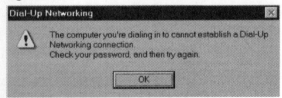

Top Tip

If after following the above procedure you fail to connect, try again. If you still do not succeed telephone your ISP or dealer helpline for further guidance. Ask them to talk you through the procedure whilst online. If you still have problems ask a computer engineer to call and help you out (get a quote first).

Section 16:
Disconnecting

Essential Information

Once you have finished surfing the Web or e-mailing you will need to disconnect. From 1998, the symbol showing that your computer is connected to the telephone network has been two linked flashing computers sitting on the taskbar. If you have a new system with the latest software this will be the symbol on your PC.

Prior to 1998, the symbol was a button on the taskbar. This will probably apply if you have an older PC with Office 97. When you are online, look at the taskbar and decide which appertains to your PC. Take either Action 1 or 2 to disconnect.

Action 1

Look at the bottom right-hand corner of your monitor. Adjacent to the digital time you will see two computers linked together and flashing. This is the connection icon (Figs. 13 and 13a).

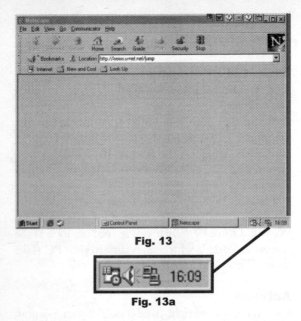

Fig. 13

Fig. 13a

Double-click on this icon and a new box will open called **Connected to My Connection**. Click on the button that says **Disconnect** (Fig. 14) and the computer will close down the telephone link to the Internet.

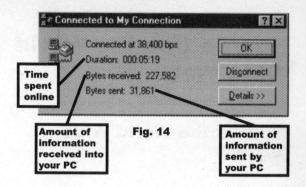

Fig. 14

Action 2

Along the taskbar you will see a button that connects to your ISP. The button will carry your username (Fig. 15).

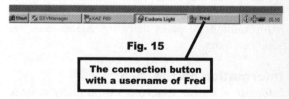

Fig. 15

The connection button
with a username of Fred

Click on this button and a box, similar to Figure 14, will open. Click once on **Disconnect** and the link to the Internet will be closed down.

Chapter Nine:
How to Use the World Wide Web

Section 1:
What is the World Wide Web?

Essential Information

The World Wide Web is a phenomenon hosted by the Internet. Imagine the Internet infrastructure like the building of a library. Information is kept on web sites instead of being held in books. A web site, like a book, is made up of individual pages. There are millions of web sites on the Internet and no one is quite sure how many millions of pages there are. Many more are added each day.

Information on the Web

Information on the Web comes from many sources, from people and organisations that wish to inform and share knowledge about their own areas of expertise. The list is huge and includes governments, research establishments, universities, schools, businesses, pressure groups, TV companies, charities, fan clubs, retail outlets, travel and entertainment guides.

The Web is truly international, so information can be sourced directly from the company or country in which you are interested.

As long as you have access to a domain (web site), anyone can create their own web page, place information upon it and then upload it onto the Internet where it can be accessed by others.

There is a large amount of excellent material out there but, just like any library, not everything is of high quality. One of the skills you will develop when using the Internet is how to sift out what you want from the enormous amount of information stored on the Web.

Section 2:
Web Addresses

Essential Information
Every web site has its own web address and each page within that site also has its own address. These addresses are a unique identification mechanism, a bit like DNA or fingerprints. There are millions of pages that are contained within the Internet and they all need to carry some special reference so that they can be identified and loaded onto your screen. These references are called Uniform Resource Locators or URLs.

Action 1

Look at this example of a web address. It is for the Imperial War Museum in London. Notice what the abbreviations stand for but don't be intimidated by them. As a beginner, just concentrate on keeping the web address accurate.

http://www.iwm.org.uk/index

http://	Hypertext Transfer Protocol
www.	World Wide Web
iwm	Organisation name
org	Type of organisation(e.g. co, com, org, gov)
uk	Country
/index	Page

Action 2

Notice the dots, colons and forward slashes. These are very important and must not be left out. There are also no spaces in the address.

Top Tip

If a Web address will not work, check that:

1. You have not left out any dots or slashes.
2. You have not added any extra dots, slashes or spaces.
3. You have not omitted a letter, e.g., og instead of org.

Section 3:
The Layout of a Web Page

Essential Information

Each web site has a **home page**. It is the home page that carries the web address, which is registered with an ISP (Internet Service Provider) and usually with an international search engine. Imagine the home page as a combination of a front cover of a book and the contents page; enticing and encouraging you to explore further and trying to keep you from disappearing onto another site! A page may contain text, graphics or pictures. It can be very simple or very detailed.

On the home page you will find various **links** that will lead you through the pages of the web site. You may have a further contents list or what is known as an image map if the site is a large one. If the site is small or easily manageable there will be links on the home page that will take you directly to other pages.

Action 1

Look at the Summersdale home page in Figure 1. This page is representative of many web sites that have similar features.

Back

Forward

The row of buttons at the top offer links which will take you deeper into the site.

Scroll bar

There are also text links in blue and underlined.

Fig. 1
The home page web address for Summersdale Publishers Ltd.

Keyword Search: Type in keywords and then click Find.

By clicking on this arrow you can scroll the page to read more information.

Action 2

Look again at Summersdale's home page in Figure 1 and find the button marked Bestsellers. By clicking on this link a new page is downloaded (Fig. 2).

Further text links take you into pages about each book.

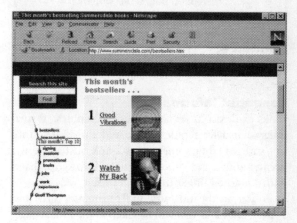

Fig. 2

By clicking on the Bestsellers button on the home page, this new page is downloaded.

Notice the web address is the same as the home page but with an addition of **/bestsellers** which identifies this particular page.

JARGON BUSTER
HTML =
Hypertext Mark-up Language
This is the language in which
most web pages are written.

Section 4:
How to Spot a Link

Essential Information

Links can exist as text, pictures or graphics. Textual links are usually in blue and are underlined. If you are not sure whether some text is a link, just move the pointer onto it and if the arrow turns into a small hand with a pointed finger then it is a link.

To activate the link, wait until the pointer turns into a hand, click and you will be taken to the linked page.

Section 5:
Links to Other Sites and Browsing the Web

Essential Information

Many web sites now dedicate a page with links to other web sites that have similar interests. If you click on these links you will be taken off the original site and on to a different site. Sometimes these can lead to dead ends with either no further links or subjects that don't interest you. Use the Back button (Fig. 1) to return to the previous site and then you can head off in a different direction. Bookmark interesting or useful sites as you go; it is easier than writing them down or trying to retrace your steps (more on Bookmarks later).

The phrase 'browsing the Web' may be an expression already familiar to you. It simply means following the links from one site to another to see what is available, like browsing along a set of books in the library. Sometimes you may stop to read an item and other times pass on by.

Action 1

In order to view the Web you need a program called a web browser. Read the following boxes to become familiar with them.

Section 6:
What are Web Browsers?

Essential Information

Microsoft Internet Explorer and Netscape Navigator are two very popular browsers; one or both of which will probably be already installed on your PC. If not, either maybe installed separately or provided by your ISP.

Fig. 3
Internet Explorer browser

Fig. 4
Netscape web browser

Action 1

Discover which web browser is on your PC and discover how to open it by following Section 7.

Section 7:
Getting onto the Web

Action 1

Depending on your ISP there may be several ways of getting onto the Web.

1. Go to **Start**, **Programs** and then look for your ISP server on the menu. Double-click and the window inviting you to log on will open.

2. You may have a shortcut icon sitting on your desktop which will lead you straight into the program if you double-click on it.

3. Alternatively, your ISP may have a menu from which you can choose the service that you require. This program will be accessed from **Start**, **Programs**, etc.

Action 2

Once you have launched the web browser, it will invite you to connect to the Internet. (Read *Chapter Eight: How to Get Connected to the Internet*, Section 15.) Before you go online, take some time to familiarise yourself with the various functions of your web browser.

Section 8:
Buttons on Internet Explorer and Netscape

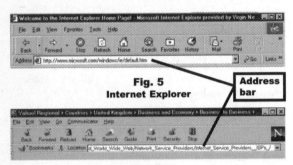

Fig. 5
Internet Explorer

Address bar

Fig. 5a
Netscape Navigator

Essential Information

There are many common elements to Netscape and Internet Explorer. Take a little time to familiarise yourself with the following before you go online.

Back and Forward: Once pages have been downloaded onto your computer it is possible to use the buttons at the top of the screen to go forward or back to pages that you have already visited. This is often quicker than using the links within the web site.

Stop: This button stops a page from downloading onto the screen. This is useful if you have dialled in the wrong web address and wish to stop the delivery of a page, or if you do not like the look of a site as it initially comes on to the screen. By using this button you can save yourself time and, of course, money, if you are paying for the Internet call.

Refresh (IE) / Reload (Netscape): This button allows you to reload an existing page onto the screen if it doesn't appear properly the first time. It gives the system a chance to locate all the information and place it in the correct order.

Print: This button allows you to print a copy of a page from a site for future reference.

Top Tip

Be aware that a page on a web site can be a lot longer than a conventional A4 sheet of paper. You could end up printing reams of paper for one tiny piece of information!

Favourites (IE) / Bookmark (Netscape): These are buttons that allow you to record the web address of a site as you browse the Web. The web address enters the computer memory and you are then able to recall it at a later date and log onto the site directly. It is a very convenient way of keeping a list of sites that you like and wish to revisit. It is also much easier than writing down the web address manually.

For more details, see Netscape Sections 9 to 12 or Internet Explorer Sections 13 to 16.

Section 9:
Bookmarks (Netscape)

Action 1

Click on Bookmarks and a drop-down menu will show a list of folders (Fig. 6).

Open a folder by clicking on it, and its contents will be displayed. These are web pages which have been automatically included in the Netscape package for your interest.

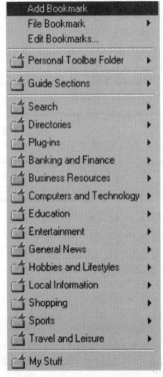

Fig. 6

290

By resting the pointer on any of these folders you will be able to see the items contained within them.

Figure 12 shows the contents of some of these folders.

Action 2
You can go straight to a web page by opening up these folders and clicking on an item whilst online.

Action 3
To add a Bookmark, go to **Bookmarks**, click once and the drop-down menu is displayed as in Figure 6.

Action 4
Click once on **Add Bookmark** and the web address of the page that you are currently viewing will be saved as a Bookmark.

Action 5
To revisit a site when you are online, open Bookmarks and click on the title of the page you want to see again. If you have stored it in a folder, open the folder first and then click on the item.

Section 10:
Creating Folders for your Bookmarks (Netscape)

Action 1

Once you have Bookmarked certain sites of interest, you may want to organise them into different subject areas. Go to **Bookmarks** and click **Edit Bookmarks** (Fig 7).

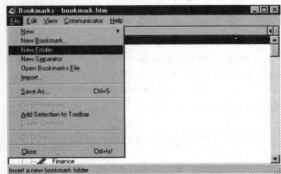

Fig. 7

On the Bookmark window that appears, click on **File** and then click on **New Folder** (Fig. 8).

Fig. 8

Press the Delete key to remove the current words 'New Folder' from the text box and then type in the new name (Fig. 9).

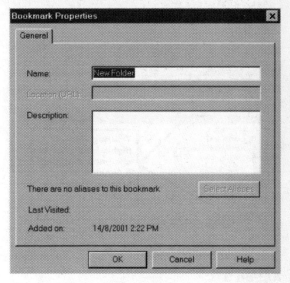

Fig. 9

Click **OK** and the new folder will appear on Bookmarks.

Action 2

If you wish to place a web page into the folder that you have created, then highlight the name of the page and then click and drag it into the new folder (Fig. 10).

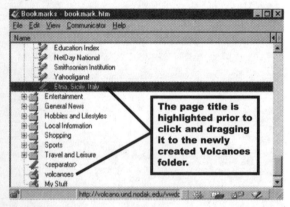

Fig. 10

Action 3

To rename a folder, go to **Bookmarks** and highlight the folder to be renamed. Go to **Edit** and click on **Bookmark Properties**.

Action 4

Bookmark Properties will show the present name of the folder highlighted. Press the Delete key and then type in the new name.

Action 5

Eventually you will wish to remove items. Go to Bookmarks and highlight the item you wish to remove. Go to **Edit** and click on **Delete** (Fig. 11).

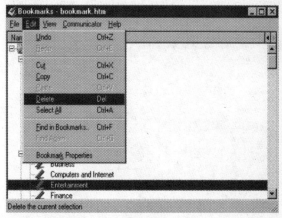

Fig. 11

To learn more about using Bookmarks, use the Help button on the Bookmark menu.

Section 11:
Saving Straight Into a Folder (Netscape)

It is possible to organise web pages straight into folders whilst online.

Action 1

Click on **Bookmark**, **File Bookmark** and then click on the folder into which you wish to file the item (Fig. 12).

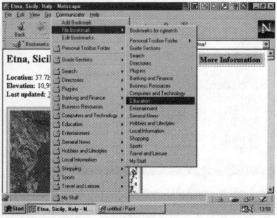

Fig. 12

The address of this web page about Etna has been recorded and filed into the Education folder.

Action 2

To return to the same web page at a later date, go to Bookmark, highlight the selected folder and the items it contains will be listed (Fig. 13). Click on your selected page whilst online.

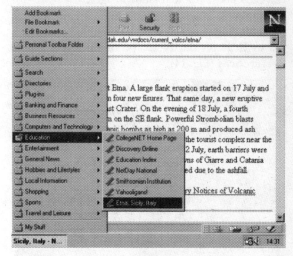

Fig. 13
The Education folder is open, showing the Etna web page. Double-clicking on the name will cause the page to be downloaded.

Section 12:
Speeding up Netscape

To speed up the rate at which pages are downloaded you can choose not to include images.

Action 1
Go to **Edit** on the Netscape menu and click on **Preferences** (Fig. 14).

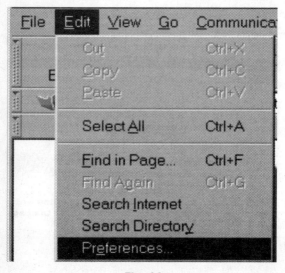

Fig. 14

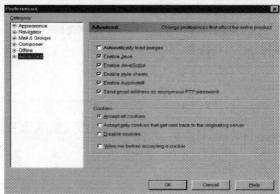

Fig. 15

Action 2

On the left-hand side is a list of folders. Click on
Advanced (Fig. 15). Click on the check box to remove
the tick by 'Automatically load images'. Click **OK**.

Action 3

If you change your mind and wish to re-include
images, just repeat the procedure but this time click
on the check box to reinstate the tick by 'Automatically
load images'. Click **OK**.

Internet Explorer (Sections 13 to 16)

On Internet Explorer, web page addresses are saved
in Favorites instead of Bookmarks. Look at Figure 5
and notice that there is the word Favorites on the menu
bar and a button called Favorites.

Section 13:
Favorites Buttons (Internet Explorer)

Action 1

Click on the word Favorites on the menu bar and a drop-down menu will appear (Fig. 16).

Fig. 16

Click on **Add to Favorites** and the Add Favourite box is displayed (Fig.17).

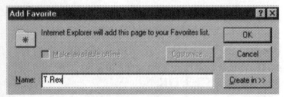

Fig. 17

This is the route that you will use to add a page of a web site to your list of Favorites – more on this later. Click **Cancel** and go on to Action 2.

Action 2

Cick on the Favorites button and the browser window
splits into two (Fig. 18).

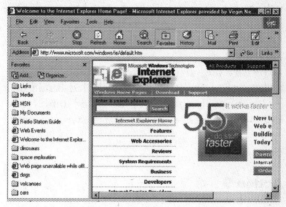

Fig. 18

Web sites that have been previously added to the list
of favourite sites are listed in alphabetical order under
My Documents.

By clicking again on Favourites so that the button
is no longer depressed, the split screen disappears and
there is more space to view a web page.

Action 3

To add a page to Favorites while you are online, go to
the word Favorites on the menu bar and the drop-

down menu appears (Fig. 16). Click on **Add Favorites** and the Add Favourite box is displayed (Fig. 17).

The name of the page that you are currently viewing will appear automatically in the text box. Click **OK** and the page will be added to Favorites.

Action 4
To revisit a site, go to the Favorites button, click once and the screen will split. Look on the left-hand panel and your web pages will be listed under My Documents. Click on the page that you wish to revisit.

or

Action 5
Click once on the word Favorites on the menu bar and the web pages will be listed either as single items or in a folder. To open a folder just click on it and the single items will be displayed. Click on the item that you wish to revisit.

Section 14:
Creating a New Folder for your Favorites (Internet Explorer)

Action 1
Click on the word Favorites on the menu bar, **Add Favorites** and the Add Favorites box appears.

Action 2
Click on **Create In** and then click on the **New Folder** button (Fig. 19).

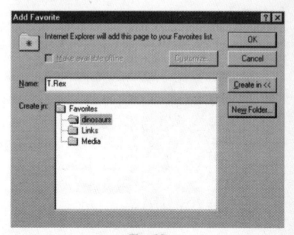

Fig. 19

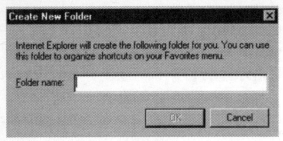

Fig. 20

Type in the name that you have chosen in the **Create New Folder** text box (Fig. 20). Click **OK**.

Action 3

Another way to create a new folder is to click on **Favorites** on the menu bar and click on **Organise Favorites**. Click on the **Create Folder** button.

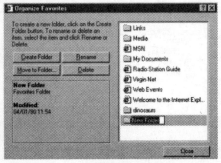

Fig. 21

A New Folder appears. Press the Delete key to remove these words and then type in the new name that you have selected.

Action 4

To move an item into a folder, click on the word **Favorites** on the menu bar, then on **Organise Favorites**. Click on the item that you wish to move to a folder and then click on the **Move to Folder** button (Fig. 21). Next, click on the folder that you want to move it to and then click **OK**.

Action 5

To rename a folder, click on **Favorites** on the menu bar, then on **Organise Favorites**. Click on the **Rename** button (Fig. 21). Delete the current name and type in the new one. Click **OK**.

Action 6

Eventually you will wish to remove items. Click on **Favorites** on the menu bar, then on **Organise Favorites**. Click on the **Delete** button (Fig. 21). A dialogue box will ask you if you wish to send the item to the Recycle Bin. Click on 'Yes' to dump, or 'No' if you've changed your mind.

Top Tip
Delete unwanted items regularly and organise the rest into logically named folders. This will save you time in searching for a specific page that you once visited.

Section 15:
Saving Straight Into a Folder (Internet Explorer)

Action 1
If you wish to place a page in a folder whilst you are online, click on **Favorites** on the menu bar, then **Add Favorites**, and then click on **Create In** (Fig. 17). A list of folders appears (Fig. 19).

Action 2
Click on the folder that you have selected. Click on **OK**. The Add Favorites box disappears and the page has been added to the folder.

To learn more about Favorites, use the Help button on the Internet Explorer menu. Click on the Index tab, type 'Favorites' into the text box and a list of subjects will appear automatically (Fig. 22). Click on the one that interests you.

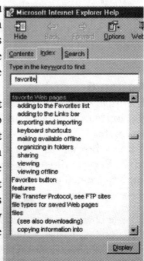

Fig. 22

Section 16:
Speeding Up Internet Explorer

To speed up the rate at which pages are downloaded you can choose not to include various images.

Action 1
Go to **Tools** on the Internet Explorer menu and click on **Internet Options** (Fig. 23).

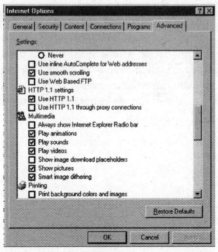

Fig. 23

Click on the **Advanced** tab. Scroll down until you reach the section called **Multimedia**. Remove the ticks in the check boxes of those items that you have decided not to download. Click on **OK**.

Action 2
If you change your mind and wish to re-include images, just repeat the procedure but this time click on the check box to reinstate the tick by those items that you have removed.

Online and Raring to Go!
Once you have connected, the first page that will appear on the screen will be your server's or browser's home page. Once the ISP's home page has downloaded you then have a choice of how to access a web site. You can either request a search tool to find it for you or, if you already know the web site address, you can go directly to it.

Section 17:
Using the Address Bar

Action 1

Type the web address into the text box on the address bar. Press Return or click on a Connect button. The Internet Service Provider then searches the whole World Wide Web (WWW) to find the correct address that you are seeking.

Once the address has been located, the pages will start to come down the 'wires' and onto the computer screen. This is called **downloading**. The first page of a web site that usually arrives onto the screen is the home page or a welcome page.

This is the welcome page of the British Manchester Terrier Club and it was accessed by typing the web address http://www.britmtclub.free-online.co.uk/ index.html
into the text
box on the
address bar and
pressing the
Return key on
the keyboard.

Fig. 24

Section 18:
Searching the Web

Essential Information

If you wish to search for a specific topic you will need to use the web search tools to help you sift through the vast array of information available. These search tools are called search engines and web directories and consist of enormous indexes and lists of web sites. They are designed to be user-friendly by categorising the web sites into various subjects and by providing a keyword search facility.

There are a number of companies who offer these facilities for free. Here is a list of some of them:

Altavista:	www.altavista.com
Excite:	www.excite.com
Infoseek:	www.infoseek.com
Lycos:	www.lycos.com
Hot Bot:	www.hotbot.com
Yahoo:	www.yahoo.com
Ask Jeeves:	www.askjeeves.co.uk
UK Directory:	www.uk.directory.co.uk
UK Plus:	www.ukplus.com
Google:	www.google.com

JARGON BUSTER
Search Engines

Enormous indexes built automatically by a computer program, which comb the Web for information. They search for compatibility with keywords.

JARGON BUSTER
Web Directories

Organised, logical lists based on a variety of chosen categories. Each category is subdivided into further groups, which are again subdivided. It is an efficient way of progressively narrowing down your search and of achieving positive, relevant results.

Section 19:
Locating Search Tools

There are generally three ways of locating a search engine or web directory: direct access, through your web browser, or through your ISP.

Direct access
In the text box on the address bar, type in the web address of the search tool and press Return on your keyboard. The home page should begin to download.

Through your web browser
Both Internet Explorer (Fig. 25) and Netscape (Fig. 26) have a search button on the web browser toolbar.

Fig. 25

To get to the search list on Internet Explorer, click on the Search icon and on the left side of the window a search directory will be listed. You can add or change the directory by clicking on Customise and choosing from the list provided.

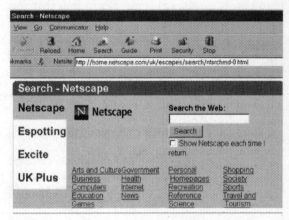

Fig. 26

Netscape will take you straight to their search tools list.

Through your ISP

There may be a search button on the home page of your ISP. Click on it and a selection of search tools will be downloaded.

Section 20:
Single Country Directories

Essential Information
Most search engines are international in their scope. If you wish to you can limit information that you access to just one country.

Action 1
Look at Figure 27. This shows the bottom section of the home page of the Excite search engine and directory. It is representative of many other search tools in allowing you to select a particular country.

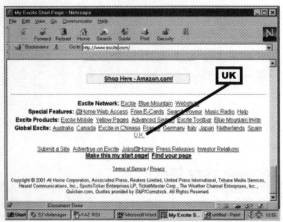

Fig. 27

314

Action 2

By clicking on UK, the Excite UK directory is downloaded (Fig. 27a) and you have access to news, interests and content deemed more relevant for a UK audience. Some search engines will display their web directories whilst others, like Excite, require you to select a directory link. Go to www.excite.com, find the link called Web Directory and click on it.

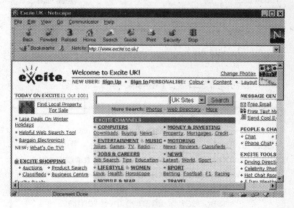

Fig. 27a
Web Directory

A Web Directory lists various categories, enabling you to target your search. You will find such directories on many of the search engines currently in operation.

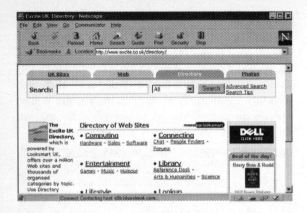

Fig. 28

Top Tip

Search Tools are not set in concrete – they evolve
and develop. Keep your eyes open for changes –
they can happen quickly in cyberspace! New tools
can be added to the market and older ones
disappear or change their format.

Section 21:
Viewing the Directory

Essential Information

When you download a search tool, the directory part
may not be immediately visible. Scroll down the home
page and you should eventually find it.

Action 1

Look at Figure 29. This shows the top section of the
home page of Yahoo UK and Ireland.

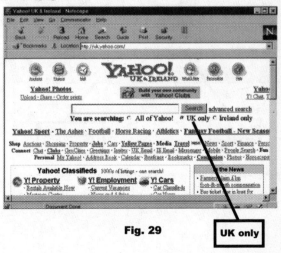

Fig. 29

UK only

317

Action 2

Scroll down the home page until you reach the directory (Fig. 30).

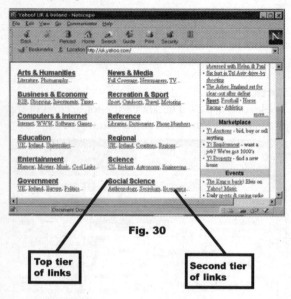

Fig. 30

Top tier of links

Second tier of links

Section 22:
How to Use a Directory

Action 1

Look again at Fig. 30. Select the top tier category, Recreation and Sport. Double-click on **Outdoors**, and a second tier of categories is downloaded and the outdoor pursuits are listed alphabetically (Fig. 31).

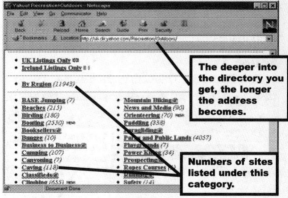

Fig. 31

Action 2

Look at the Canyoning category. The number by the side indicates the number of web sites listed; seven in this case. Double-click on **Canyoning** and the titles of all those sites will be listed. Double-click on any title that interests you and that web site will be downloaded.

Section 23:
Searching Using Keywords

Essential Information

Most search engines and many directories will provide a keyword search facility. When you type in your keywords the search engine will attempt to match them to words in a web site title or in the contents of the first page. Very often a single word will find what you want. If you need to use more than one word, always type them in the descending order of importance.

Action 1

Look at Figure 32. This is the search engine Lycos.

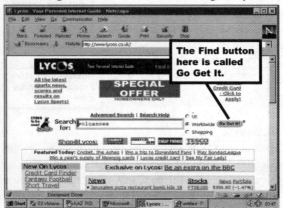

Fig. 32

The word 'volcano' was typed into the Keyword box and then the search button was single-clicked. The search was for the whole of Lycos and not confined to a single country.

Over 252,900 results!

Ten sites are listed on one page. Click on **Next** at the bottom of the page to view the next 10. However, 252,900 results are going to take a long time to work through!

The search needs to be narrowed.

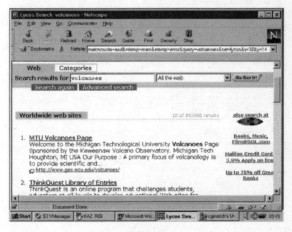

Fig. 33
First 10 of 252,900 results.

Action 2

Look at Figure 34. The search was narrowed by typing 'volcano etna' into the text box, the words in descending order of importance.

This has reduced the number of sites. Those sites that have the best matches to the keywords are always listed first. So the first 10–20 will be the most relevant. By the way, a search for just 'etna' produced a pop group and a metal company, but no volcano!

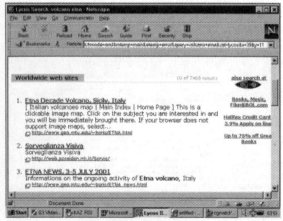

Fig. 34

Section 24:
Searching for a Specific Phrase

It is possible to find a site using a specific phrase. Type the phrase into the keyword text box on the search tool that you have chosen and be sure to place it in quotation marks. The following is an example using the search engine AltaVista.

Action 1
Look at Figure 35. In the **Find This** text box is "I have a dream". The Search button was clicked.

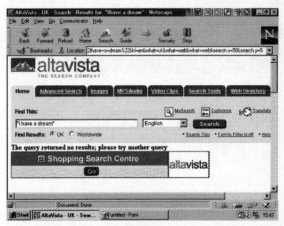

Fig. 35

Action 2

Look at Figure 36. AltaVista found a number of relevant sites, including one about Martin Luther King, who originated the phrase.

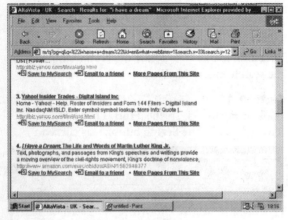

Fig. 36

Section 25:
Safety and Security on the Internet

Netscape offers the user unrestricted access to the Internet. This means that if you wish to prevent the downloading of inappropriate material you will need to install your own 'nanny' program (see below).

Microsoft Internet Explorer offers advice on safety and security. To find out more, open up Internet Explorer and click on the Help button.

Subjects listed are:

Sending Information on the Internet Safely

Protecting your Computer Whilst Online

Controlling Access to Inappropriate Internet Content.

Internet Service Providers
Some ISPs offer Internet safety as part of their service. For example, BT Internet includes Cyber Patrol as part of their package. More ISPs are now aware of the need for filtering information to make it acceptable for family viewing and are seeking to provide customers with integral programs that take care of the supervision of web sites. If you want such a service, remember to ask before you sign up.

Software Programmes Available

There are software programmes available independently of your ISP. These programs work behind the scenes scanning all pages for unacceptable content.

Go online to get more information:

Net Nanny: http://www.netnanny.com/home.html
Cyber Patrol (offers free trial download): http://www.cyberpatrol.com

Online Banking and Online Shopping

Great strides have been made in security over the Internet and online banking and shopping are now a fact of life. The encoding devices used are of the highest quality in the effort to maintain security.

However, when shopping online, only ever shop on secure sites. Once you click on a shopping page you should be told that you are about to enter a secure site (Fig. 37).

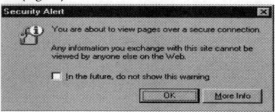

Fig. 37

If you are not sure whether or not the site is secure, look for the padlock on your web browser. On Netscape it is in the bottom left-hand corner (Fig. 38) and on Internet Explorer it is in the bottom right (Fig. 38a)

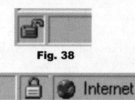

Fig. 38

Fig. 38a

If the site that you are visiting is secure then the little padlock will be closed. If the site is not secure then the padlock will be open as in Figure 38. In such a case it may be advisable to consider other ways of making payment.

Another way of telling is to look at the http:// part of the web address. If the site is secure it becomes https:// (Fig. 39).

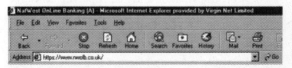

Fig. 39

Section 26:
Other Internet Services

Downloading Pages for Offline Viewing

Open up Netscape and click on the **Help** button. Click on **Contents** and then **About Netcaster** on the left panel. About Netcaster will tell you about downloading files and offline browsing.

Alternatively, open up Internet Explorer. Click on the **Help** button and then on the **Index** tab. Type 'Downloading Web Pages' into the text box and a list of relevant items will appear in the column below.

Discussion Groups and Newsgroups

Netscape Navigator has a newsreader and mail program but they have to be configured before they can be used. To do this, open the main Netscape window, click on **Edit** and then on **Preferences**. Open the folder called **Mail and Groups** on the left panel of the window and work your way through the instructions.

For more information and help, open up Netscape and click on **Help**. Click on **Overview** on the panel on the left of the window. Click on **Using Discussion Groups**.

Alternatively, open up Internet Explorer and click on the **Help** button. Click on the **Index** tab and in the text box type in the word 'Newsgroups'. A list of relevant items will appear. Click on one that is appropriate.

More information is available from:

Usenet Information Center Launch Pad:

> http://sunsite.unc.edu/usenet-i

What is Usenet?:

> http://www.sans.vuw.ac.nz/sans/usemet.html

Internet Chat

Chat rooms are places where like-minded people can exchange news and views on the Internet. Chat rooms are often listed on the home page of an ISP or a search engine or directory. Information is also available online.

Try:
http://www.yahoo.com/Computers_and_Internet
/Internet/Chatting.

Various online companies have chat rooms. You can also access networks that host Internet Relay Chat (IRC). IRC enables you to 'chat' in real time (i.e. as soon as you have typed your message). This is done through a server. Whichever server you use will dictate which IRC network that you join.

Information is available online. Try:

www.bbc.co.uk/webwise/guides/mirc/mircl.shtml

or

http://www2.undernet.org/~cs93jtl/IRC.html

Top Tip

Treat Internet chatting with extreme caution and remember that people are not always what they pretend to be. It is advisable not to let children or vulnerable people use chat rooms or have access to IRC.

TV Chat

Many TV companies now attach an online chat service to some of their popular programmes. These allow you to participate in interviewing experts and personalities about subjects broadcast on TV programmes.

Section 27:
A Selection of Web Sites

There are literally millions of web sites on the Internet. Here are a few to start you off on your Internet odyssey! All of them begin with **http://** so make sure that this is present in the web browser address bar before you type in the rest of the address. There are a few addresses included which do not contain www – this is not a printing mistake, the letters are simply not required for that particular address. For example: http://members.aol.com/vetadviceforfree.

Happy browsing!

Sport

Tennis:	www.wimbledon.com
Football:	www.soccernet.com
Golf:	www.golf.com
General:	www.english.sports.gov.uk
Rugby:	www.rfl.uk.com
Cricket:	www.cricket.org

Museums and Military History

Imperial War Museum:	www.iwm.org.uk
Commonwealth War Graves:	www.cwgc.org.uk
Army Records Society:	www.armyrecordssociety.org.uk
National Army Museum:	www.national-army-museum.ac.uk/index.html
Battle of Britain:	www.raf.mod.uk/bob1940/

British Library: www.bl.uk
Victoria and Albert Museum: www.vam.ac.uk
Bodlian Library: www.bodley.ox.ac.uk
British Museum: www.british-museum.ac.uk
National Maritime Museum: www.port.nmm.ac.uk

Government and Royalty

British Monarchy: www.royal.gov.uk
Royal Collection: www.the-royal-collection.org.uk
Prince of Wales: www.princeofwales.gov.uk
Royal genealogical data:
www.dcs.hull.ac.uk/public/genealogyGEDCOM.html
10 Downing Street: www.number-10.gov.uk
European Parliament: www.europarl.org.uk
The White House: www.whitehouse.gov/

Travel

Travellersweb: www.travellersweb.com
Railtrack: www.railtrack.com
Cheap flights: www.cheapflights.com

Books

Amazon Books: www.amazon.co.uk
The Children's Bookshop: www.childrensbookshop.com
J.R.R. Tolkein: http://gollum.usask.ca/tolkien/index.html
Terry Pratchet: www.us.lspace.org/
Harry Potter: www.hpnews.co.uk
and www.harrypotter.warnerbros.co.uk

On-line encyclopaedia: www.britannica.com
Travel Books: www.travel-bookshop.com

Newspapers and Magazines

British Library: www.bl.uk/collections/newspaper
Financial Times: www.ft.com
The Guardian: www.guardian.co.uk
The Times: www.the-times.co.uk
Sport: www.sportfirst.com
Internet Magazine: www.netmag.co.uk
Gardens Illustrated: www.gardensillustrated.com

Genealogy

Society of Genealogy: www.sog.org.uk
Genuki: www.gold.ac.uk/genuki
Institute of Genealogy and Historic Studies:
                         www.hgs.ac.uk
Record Office for Scotland:
     http://wood.ccta.gov.uk/grosweb/grosearch.nsf
Rootsweb: www.rootsweb.com/
Public Record Office: www.pro.gov.uk

Science

The Science Museum: www.sciencemuseum.org.uk
The Smithsonian Institute: www.si.edu
Nasa Earth Observatory: www.earthobservatory.nasa.gov/
The Met Office: www.met-office.gov.uk

British Space Agency:	www.bnsc.gov.uk
Nasa:	www.nasa.gov/
Exploratorium Observatory:	www.exploratorium.edu

Environment

The National Trust:	www.nationaltrust.org.uk
Greenpeace:	www.greenpeace.org.uk
Eden Project:	www.edenproject.com
Friends of the Earth:	www.foe.co.uk
Plantlife:	www.plantlife.org.uk
The Forestry Commission:	www.forestry.gov.uk
The Wildlife Trust:	www.wildlifetrust.org.uk/

Art and Entertainment

National Gallery:	www.nationalgallery.org.uk
Tate Gallery:	www.tate.org.uk
Internet Movies Database:	www.imdb.com
British Film Institute:	www.bfi.co.uk
BBC:	www.bbc.co.uk
Channel 4:	www.channel4.com
ITV:	www.itv.co.uk
Sky:	www.sky.com

Chapter Ten:
How to Use E-mail

Essential Information

E-mail is short for 'electronic mail'. It allows information to be sent anywhere in the world from one computer to another via the telephone system. It is particularly useful for contacting people abroad or sending short messages. E-mail programs are all very similar in the various functions they offer.

JARGON BUSTER
Snail Mail
The traditional postal service has been dubbed 'snail mail' because of its relative slowness of delivery in comparison with the speed of e-mail.

Section 1:
Choosing an E-mail Program

Essential Information
There are various e-mail programs to choose from. If you are buying a new computer, an Internet system with e-mail may be included as part of the software. If you are not yet on the Internet then you will need to select an Internet Service Provider (ISP) who will include an e-mail facility with the package that you choose. (If you skipped over the Internet section, go back and read it, as the information is relevant to e-mailing.) One of the programs below may be the one used by your ISP or installed on your PC. You can also download programs from the Internet; you do not have to stick to just one system.

Here are four examples of e-mail programs:

Outlook Express
– This should be installed along with Internet Explorer and is the system we will cover.

Eudora Light

– This free e-mail program can be downloaded from http://www.eudora.com

Netscape

– A free e-mail program that can be downloaded from http://home.netscape.com

Hotmail

– A very popular e-mail service. Information is available from http://www.hotmail.com

As well as an Internet Service Provider you will also need an internal or external modem connected to your computer (for more information read *Chapter Eight: How to Get Connected to the Internet*, Section 3) and a 'plug in' telephone connection.

Section 2:
E-mail Addresses

Essential Information

To send and receive e-mails you must have an e-mail address, just as you need a home address to receive traditional post. Each e-mail address is unique, like your home address. If you do not want to use your full name on the address you can always choose a nickname – as long as you don't forget what it is!

Action 1

Look at the sample e-mail address below. Notice that the address is all in lower-case letters and includes dots (or full stops) which are very important. The e-mail address will not operate if you leave them out. There are also no spaces between words.

The e-mail address contains certain parts:

> Your name
> The symbol @ meaning 'at'
> The name of your service provider
> .co or .com
> A code representing your country

fredsmith@serviceprovider.co.uk

A commercial organisation will use either '.co' or '.com', depending on the country. In Britain, '.co' is normally used.

Action 2

Look at the e-mail address below. Outside America a code is used to represent a country. If Fred Smith lived in *Au*stralia his e-mail address might be:
fredsmith@serviceprovider.co.au

Section 3:
Setting Up E-mail

Essential Information

Once you have selected an e-mail program it will need to be set up (configured). Before you start, make sure that you have the following information ready:

> Username
> Password
> Your chosen e-mail name
> E-mail address

> Any other details your ISP may have given you about your account.

Configuring or setting up the e-mail is done by a **Wizard**, which will request certain details from you and then make the mail connection. The Wizard will lead you through the procedure.

Action 1

Follow the instructions but if you are unsure about some of the checkboxes then leave them alone and the computer will set their defaults. What you must fill in are details about your e-mail account and your service provider.

Action 2

Any problems? This is where your ISP telephone helpline comes in handy. Tell them your difficulty and ask them to take you through the procedure from the beginning. It really does save a lot of hassle! If you do not have a helpline, try again. If you really are stuck, ask a qualified engineer to assist (you can find them in the telephone book but get a quote first). Once the settings have been made (configured) you will be ready to send and receive your e-mail messages.

Section 4:
Opening your E-mail Program

Essential Information

Once your program has been set up there could be two ways of opening it. Whilst installing your Internet or e-mail program a shortcut may have been created. This icon will sit on the desktop. The other way to access your e-mail is by going through Programs.

Action 1

Double-click on the icon on your desktop and the e-mail program opens.

Alternatively, if no shortcut has been created then you need to go to **Start** on the taskbar, click once to open the menu and highlight **Programs**. Another drop-down menu will appear listing all the programs on the computer. Look for the name of your e-mail program and single-click.

Section 5:
Connecting

The connecting procedure is the same for e-mailing as it is for using the Internet. If you have forgotten how to do this, refer back to page 271.

Section 6:
Working Offline

Essential Information
It is a good idea to compose your e-mail offline, especially if you have a number of messages to write. Outlook Express can store and queue messages, ready to be sent when you next go online. You will discover how to do this later in this chapter.

JARGON BUSTER
Offline
Not connected to the telephone network.

Section 7:
The E-mail Window

Action 1
Once you have opened Outlook Express, look at the
e-mail window. Notice the buttons along the top of
the window, just below the menu bar and locate the
functions illustrated in Figure 1.

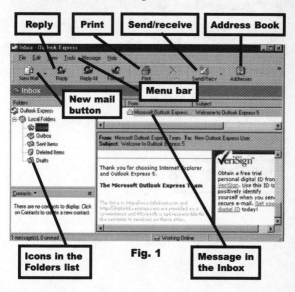

Fig. 1

343

The left panel illustrated in Figure 1 may not resemble the picture on your e-mail window. Don't worry! It simply means that your e-mail has not yet been customised. You can leave the panel as it is or if you would like to change it follow the steps in Section 8.

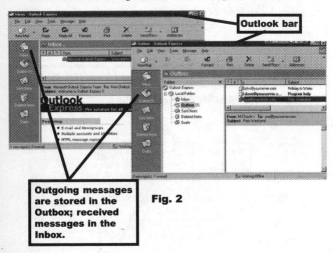

Outlook bar

Outgoing messages are stored in the Outbox; received messages in the Inbox.

Fig. 2

Section 8:
Customising the E-mail Window

Action 1
Click on **View** on the menu bar and a drop-down menu appears. Click on **Layout** (Fig. 3).

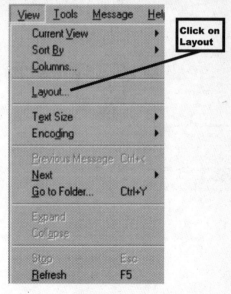

Fig. 3

Action 2

The **Window Layout Properties** box opens as in Figure 4.

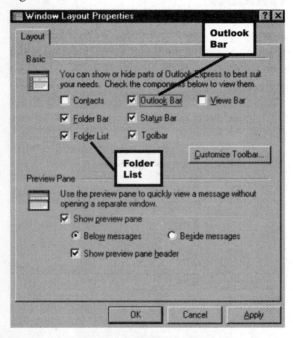

Fig. 4

Action 3

If you only want the **Outlook Bar** visible (Fig. 2), make sure that a tick is present in the check box by 'Outlook Bar' on the window Layout Properties (Fig. 4). If it is not, just move the pointer onto the check box and click once. Then make sure that the tick in the check box by the side of Folders list is removed. Click on **Apply**, then **OK**.

Action 4

If you only want the Folders List (Fig. 2), remove the tick in the check box by 'Outlook Bar' and make sure that there is a tick in the checkbox by **Folders List**.

Action 5

If you want both the Outlook Bar and the Folders List visible (Fig. 2), make sure that there are ticks in the check boxes by the side of each.

Section 9:
Writing a Message

Action 1

Click on **New Mail** (Fig. 1). Look at the first part of the message window (Fig. 5).

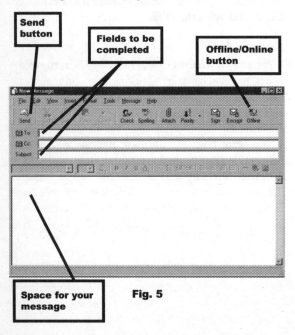

Fig. 5

The window contains various sections or fields that need to be completed in order to send a message. To type inside a field, move the pointer onto the relevant place and click once. The text cursor will appear and you will be able to type.

To: Type the recipient's e-mail address.
Subject: Give your message a short relevant subject.

Ignore the following field for the moment:
Cc: Carbon copy (more in Section 18).

There is no **From** field with Outlook Express. This is dealt with automatically by the program so that your own e-mail address will appear on your recipient's e-mail message.

Action 2
The large space in the bottom half of the window is where you type your message. Move your pointer here (Fig. 5), click once and you can begin to type.

Section 10:
Sending E-mail

Essential Information
Once you have finished writing your message and filling in the relevant fields, you will need to go online to send your e-mail. If you wish to store your message and send it later, read Section 16.

Action 1
If you cannot remember how to log on, refer back to page 271. Once you have logged on, simply click on the **Send** button on the message window (Fig. 5), and your e-mail will be immediately sent.

Section 11:
Receiving E-mail

Essential Information
It is possible to customise Outlook Express to ring up at various times and check whether you have any messages to download. However, it is probably best if you keep control of the telephone yourself and check for mail whenever you decide to go online.

Action 1

Go to **Tools** on the menu bar, click once and then click on **Options**. The Options box opens (Fig. 6). Select the tab called **General**.

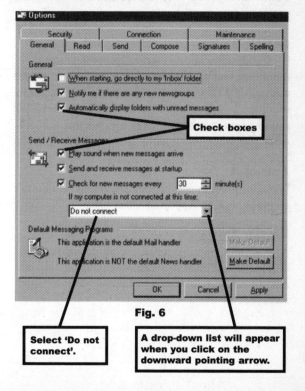

Fig. 6

Select 'Do not connect'.

A drop-down list will appear when you click on the downward pointing arrow.

351

Action 2

Click on the drop-down list indicated in Figure 6 and select 'Do not connect'. This means that you will have control over when to go online and not the e-mail program.

Action 3

Look at the check boxes on the Options box and select those that you wish to keep. Remember that if you wish to keep a function there must be a tick present in the check box. It is probably a good idea to select 'Play sound when new messages arrive', because this will make you aware when you have new mail.

Action 4

When you have finished making your selections, don't forget to click on **Apply** and then **OK**.

Action 5

To receive new mail, click on the **Send/Receive** button. Select from the drop-down menu **Receive All**. If you also have messages to send, click on **Send/Receive**.

Section 12:
The Inbox

Essential Information
Once your e-mails have been downloaded they are stored in the Inbox. Look at Figure 1 and notice that the Inbox icon has been selected and that the right-hand panel lists all the e-mails that have been received. At the moment only one e-mail message is listed; a welcome message from Microsoft.

Action 1
Click on the Inbox icon or the Inbox button as in Figures 1 and 2. The Inbox opens and the messages that it contains are listed on the right (Fig. 1).

Action 2
To open a message, move the pointer on to the relevant single line entry and double-click and the message will be displayed.

Section 13:
Replying to E-mail

Essential Information
You can reply to a message that has just been received or to a previous message stored in the Inbox. Using this system helps the recipient to remember the purpose and content of the original message because the original message appears underneath yours. It also saves you having to type in the recipient's e-mail address!

Action 1
Click on the **Reply** button along the top of the e-mail window just below the menu bar (Fig. 1). The sender's e-mail address is automatically inserted into the new e-mail message window and the original message is copied.

Action 2
Type in your own message, retaining any of the key points of the sender's message that you wish to include. Any text not required can be deleted.

Action 3
Log on and click on the **Send** button.

Section 14:
The Outbox

Essential Information

Outlook Express keeps a record in the Outbox of all the e-mails that you have sent. These are shown as single line entries in the same way as your incoming messages are listed in the Inbox. Look at Figure 2 and notice that the Outbox button is highlighted and on the right of the e-mail window are listed all the messages that have so far been sent.

When you queue messages they are kept in the Outbox until you are ready to send them. These e-mails are easy to spot as they will have a Q by the side of them.

Action 1

To open the Outbox, click on the Outbox icon or the button on the Outlook bar. To open an outgoing message, click on the single line entry to highlight, then double-click. Your message will open.

Section 15:
Deleting

Essential Information
It is not necessary to retain all the messages that you send or receive. It is possible to remove unwanted messages from both the Outbox and the Inbox. It is a good idea to regularly tidy up your mailboxes!

Action 1
Select whichever mailbox you are going to tidy.

Action 2
Highlight the e-mail to be removed by clicking once (Fig. 7) and then go to **Edit** on the menu bar and click on **Delete** (Fig. 8).

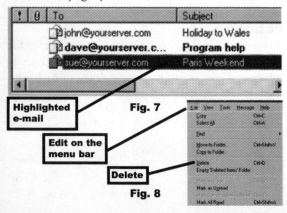

356

Section 16:
Queuing Messages

You may wish to queue your messages to be sent at a later date.

Action 1
To work offline, simply click on the **Offline/Online** button so that it shows 'Offline' (Fig. 5). Type your message in the normal way and then click on **Send**.

Action 2
The **Send Mail** box will appear (Fig. 9). Click **OK**.

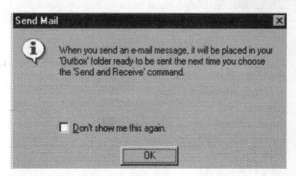

Send Mail   ☒

ⓘ When you send an e-mail message, it will be placed in your
    'Outbox' folder ready to be sent the next time you choose
    the 'Send and Receive' command.

☐ Don't show me this again.

[OK   ]

Fig. 9

Action 3
When you next go online simply click on the **Send/Receive** button and the message will be sent.

Section 17:
Attaching Documents or Files

It is possible to attach documents or files held on your computer to an e-mail. It is often quicker and cheaper than sending them by post. However, if your files are large or include graphics or pictures they may take a long time to get through. They will also take the recipient a long time to download.

Action 1
Click on the **Attach** button (it looks like a paperclip) or go to **Insert** and click on **File Attachment** (Fig. 10).

Fig. 10

Action 2
A box opens called **Insert Attachment**. Locate and select your document, click **OK** and the document is attached to the e-mail (Fig. 11).

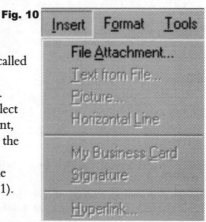

Insert	Format	Tools
File Attachment...		
Text from File...		
Picture...		
Horizontal Line		
My Business Card		
Signature		
Hyperlink...		

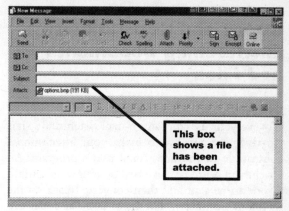

This box shows a file has been attached.

Fig. 11

Section 18:
Sending Messages to Several People

Look at Figure 11 and notice a field in the top part of the window called **Cc** (carbon copy). To send a message to several people, type one address in the **To** field and the rest in the **Cc** field. Separate them by a semicolon and a space. When your e-mail is sent, each person will receive a copy of the message and they will all be able to see who else received a copy.

Section 19:
Codes and Compatibility in Attaching Documents and Files

Essential Information

Not everyone uses the same e-mail system and so it is worth knowing how to make your attachments compatible to another e-mail user's program. An attachment has to be converted by your e-mailer into a code to be sent and then converted back by the recipient's e-mailer. The most popular codes are UUEncode, MIME and Binhex.

If your recipient is unable to read your attachment, check that you are both using the same code. If you are not compatible, it is usually possible to change. If you are using Outlook Express, phone the Microsoft helpline for guidance.

Section 20:
E-mail Address Books

Essential Information
Most e-mail programs have address books that can be used to store e-mail addresses. It's probably quicker to request your e-mail program to enter the recipient's address than for you to type it manually. Although all e-mail programs follow a similar pattern they can be different in the formatting of their address books.

Action 1
To discover how your address book works, open up your e-mail program, click on **Help** on the menu bar, locate **Topics** and search for **Address Book**.

Section 21:
E-mail Etiquette, Abbreviations and Emoticons

Essential Information
1. Keep your message short and to the point. Remember, someone else has got to pay to download your piece of prose!
2. E-mails are not conventional letters so you don't

need to write it like one with your home address or
the date.

3. DON'T SHOUT! That is, do not type your
message in capital letters.

4. Give your message a subject; it helps the recipient
to manage their files.

5. Remember that your e-mails can be read by anyone
who has access to your computer so be polite and
discrete.

6. Once an e-mail has been sent it enters the public
domain. It could then be forwarded by your recipient
onto others, so only include material or information
that you don't mind the rest of the world knowing.

Abbreviations and **emoticons** were originally
developed when messages had to be composed online
and time was of the essence. Now they are not so
necessary but have become part of e-mail culture.

Abbreviations
Here are some common abbreviations in e-mails:

BTW:	By the way
FYI:	For your information
FAQ:	Frequently asked questions
IMHO:	In my humble opinion
TIA:	Thanks in advance
IOW:	In other words

Smilies are little pictures that help to convey meaning to your e-mail. They are also called emoticons. Use the normal letters and symbols on the keyboard, like colons, semicolons, and brackets, to create the following examples of smilies:

:-) Happy   :-(Sad   :-II Angry

;-) Wink   :-D Laughing   :-I Not amused

If you can't see the connection between the smiley and its meaning, turn the page sideways.

Section 22:
Printing an E-mail

Action 1
To print a copy of an e-mail, look along the top of the e-mail window and locate a button with a picture of a small printer.

Action 2
Click once on the button and the **Print** box will appear. See page 139 for details on how to print.

Action 3
Select how many copies you want and the print range. Click **OK**.

Chapter Eleven:
How to Keep Your Computer Healthy

Section 1:
Cleanliness and The Computer System

Essential Information

Cleanliness is an important aspect of computer usage. The computer and all its components are pieces of high-tech electronic equipment and two of its greatest enemies are dirt and dust.

It is with this in mind that the systems unit is designed to be insulated against outside interference. However, it is still possible to 'inject' dust into the system via the floppy disk and the CD/DVD drive.

Consequently, disks should be kept as clean as possible. This will help to maintain a healthy computer and also protect the information that is stored on your disks. Dust or grit within the floppy can damage it irreparably and likewise fingermarks or dirt on a CD.

Action 1

Store your floppy disks in a clean and dust-free environment. Never put them loose in your pocket or bag. If you need to carry them about with you, at least keep them in an envelope. CDs should always be held by the edges and stored in the wallet or case provided when not in use. Keep your systems unit free from dust. Special wipes to clean the systems unit are available from your local computer store or use a dust-free cloth.

Top Tip
Don't forget to clean your monitor screen. It is not good for your eyesight to be peering at the screen through a fog!

Section 2:
Tidiness

Essential Information
Computer tidiness begins once you start creating documents and saving them onto floppy disks and the hard drive. If you fail to organise you may find that you've forgotten under what names you saved a document, your computer tells you that it is running out of space, or that you have hundreds of unnamed floppy disks.

Action 1

You need to tidy and manage your documents and files. Read *Chapter Seven: How to Create and Manage Files* and then set aside some time to get yourself organised!

Action 2

If your computer has a small amount of memory, it may be a good idea to check how much space is left. Read Section 9 about DriveSpace and the Compression Agent.

Section 3:
Computer Viruses: Prevention

There are three ways of acquiring an unwelcome computer virus:

1. They can come attached to e-mails.

2. They can come on floppy disks that have been used on another computer.

3. They can be downloaded from an unsecured site on the World Wide Web (although your ISP will run checks on all material).

JARGON BUSTER
Virus

A virus is a piece of code attached to a program. Once the virus infects a computer it can corrupt the programs on the system and either be just an irritant or very damaging, depending on the nature of the virus.

Action 1

If you receive an e-mail from someone you do not know and it has an attachment, the best thing to do with it is place it unopened in the Recycle Bin or delete it completely from your system.

JARGON BUSTER
Backup Disks

Keep a copy of your important files on a floppy disk or a CD. If anything happens to your PC's hard drive, then you will not have lost all your work.

Action 2

Do not interchange floppy disks between home and the workplace as this is a common way of introducing and spreading viruses.

Section 4:
Computer Viruses: Cure

Essential Information

All owners of computers should invest in an anti-virus program. It will sit there behind the scenes waiting for you to scan a file or program for a virus.

Action 1

Acquire an anti-virus program. There are a number on the market available on floppy and CD from your local computer store.

Place the disk in the computer and follow the instructions as they appear on your screen.
Some programs can be downloaded from the Internet, for example: Norton Antivirus from: http://www.symantic.com/avcenter/index.html and McAfee Virus Scan from: http://www.mcafee.com.

There are many more anti-virus programs on the Internet so if you want to check them out, type 'anti-virus' in the text box on your search engine.

Action 2

Be aware of the files and programs that should be scanned by your anti-virus program. These are:
1. Any files or programs that have attachments.
2. Any files or programs that have 'macro programs'

(small programs that work within a program).

Your virus-checking program will tell you whenever it detects a virus and can usually 'kill' any it finds at the touch of a button. It only takes a few moments to scan a file, so if in doubt, check!

Top Tip

Get the latest version of anti-virus programs, as they will be able to deal with the most recent releases of virus. If you do get a virus that conventional anti-virus programs cannot deal with, you can return your new computer to your dealer who will wipe the hard disk clean but you will lose all work saved onto the hard disk. Keep a backup of all important information.

Section 5:
How to Escape or Close Down

When you are busy working on the computer you may sometimes, without realising, open up too many windows or programs on the screen. Sometimes this may cause the computer to jam.

The possible consequences are:

1. The screen may freeze.

2. The mouse may stop working.

3. It may not be possible to close down any windows.

4. You may be left with a screen full of material and no way of extricating yourself from the jam.

Action 1
You will need to escape from this situation and close down. The keyboard is able to provide you with an alternative way of moving around the screen.

Look at your keyboard and identify these keys:

> **Control (Ctrl),**
>
> **Escape (Esc),**
>
> **Cursor (arrow) keys,**
>
> **Tab Key,**
>
> **Return.**

Action 2

Press **Control**, and whilst holding the key down, press **Escape**. The menu from the Start button should appear. Use the cursor key to highlight **Shutdown** and when Shutdown is highlighted, press Return. The **Shutdown Windows** box will appear. Use the cursor keys to select **Shutdown Computer** and use the tab key to select 'Yes', then press Return. The computer may (if you're lucky) ask you if you want to save your work. Use the tab key to select 'Yes'. Once it has saved any files, the computer will proceed to close down.

Alternatively, you can press **Control**, **Alt** (next to the space bar) and **Delete** at the same time. This will automatically shut down your computer but you will not have the option of saving your work.

Top Tip

Always save your work as you go along. You never know when the computer may jam, a power cut or power surge may occur or even when someone may accidentally pull out the PC plug! These things DO happen!

Section 6:
Autofix Programs for Microsoft Office 2000 and Works 2000

Essential Information

The Autofix program can be used if you are working on a particular program and a problem arises such as the mouse pointer freezing, the program jamming or a window opening in front of your work saying 'You have committed an illegal act'.

Action 1

Click on **Help** on the menu bar and click once on **Detect and Repair**. A box opens telling you that 'Detect and Repair will automatically find and fix errors in this application'. It will also ask you to provide various pieces of information and to exit or open applications. Finally there is a check box asking if you want the computer shortcuts whilst repairing. Click once on **Start** and wait for further instructions.

Action 2

If you find this does not cure the problem then it may pay you to try putting your hard disk through the **Defragmenting** and **ScanDisk** programs.

Section 7:
Autofix Programs to Purchase

If you do not have the Microsoft Autofix program, or if you find that it does not always solve a problem, then it may be a good idea to purchase additional help. There are a variety of programs available on CD that you can load into the CD tray and then follow the instructions. The program will sit behind the scenes working and fixing problems as they arise. Two examples of these are **First Aid** and **Oil Change**. Any good computer store will be able to provide you with these types of programs.

Section 8:
System Tools: Defragmenting

Essential Information

When you save a document or file onto your hard disk a certain amount of space is taken up. When you delete and add to a document and save it again on your hard disk, the computer will fill up the first space and then put the rest elsewhere. Over a long period, your document could, in theory, be saved in fragments in dozens of spaces on your hard disk. This will slow down the operation of the computer.

Defragmenting collects all these pieces of your document and puts them in one place again on the hard disk.

Action 1

To run your defragmenting program, go to **Start** and click once, then highlight **Programs**, **Accessories**, **System Tools** and then click once on **Disk Defragmenter** (Fig. 1).

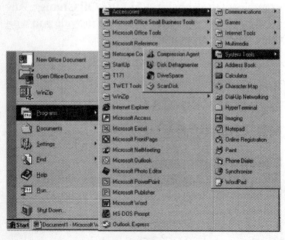

Fig. 1

Action 2

A new box will open called **Select Drive** (Fig. 2).

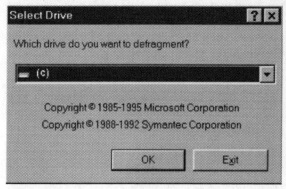

Fig. 2

This window asks you to select which drive you want to defragment. Select your hard disk and then click on **OK**. A new box will open called **Disk Defragmenter** (Fig. 3).

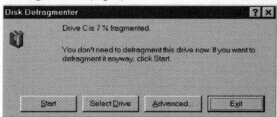

Fig. 3

At the top of this window there is a message stating
how much of the drive is defragmented and whether
you need to defragment now. Decide what you want
to do and if you still want to defragment, click once
on **Start**. A new box will open called **Defragmenting
Drive C** (Fig. 4) showing you how far the
defragmenting process has got.

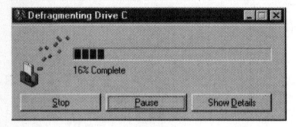

Fig. 4

Just sit back and wait for the computer to finish.

Section 9:
System Tools: DriveSpace and Compression Agent

Essential Information

DriveSpace allows you to check the amount of space on your hard drive. The Compression Agent is a means of reducing the amount of space taken up and thereby increasing the amount of available free space on the hard drive.

Top Tip

If you have a computer with a small amount of memory and you keep adding a lot of programs then it is a good idea to use DriveSpace to check the amount of room left on the hard drive. Use the Compression Agent to compress the programs so that you have more space available.

Action 1

To open DriveSpace, click once on **Start** on the taskbar, highlight **Programs**, **Accessories** then **System Tools** and click once on **DriveSpace**. A box opens called DriveSpace (Fig. 5).

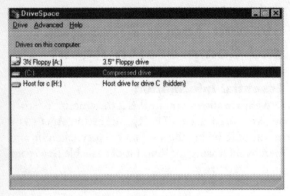

Fig. 5

Action 2

Double-click on hard drive (C) and a new window opens called **Compression Properties Drive C** (see Fig. 6). A disk at the bottom of this box will show you how much of your hard drive has been used and how much is still free. Above the disk is the actual free space in megabytes. Free space is in one colour and used space in another. Decide whether you need more space on your drive and then close this box by clicking on the cross in the Close box or click on **OK**. You are returned to the DriveSpace box.

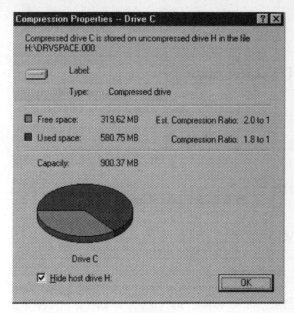

Fig. 6

Action 3

Click on **Drive** on the menu bar and a drop-down menu appears offering various options (Fig. 7). If you wish to compress the drive, click on **Compress** and go to Action 4. If you decide not to compress, close the DriveSpace window by clicking on the cross in the Close box.

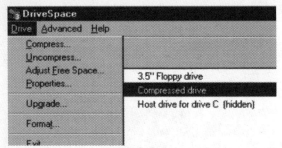

Fig. 7

Action 4

A new box will open called **Compression Agent**. It can take a long time to compress your files so make sure that it is convenient for you to do so. Read and follow the instructions on the box and then click on **Start** (Fig. 8).

Action 5

While the Compression Agent is working, a blue status bar will be visible, showing how far the process has progressed. It will also tell you how much disk space has been gained. In Figure 9, over 60 MB of space has been gained. Click on **Exit** when the compression is completed.

Action 6

It is also possible on Office 2000 and Works 2000 to access the Compression Agent straight from the systems tools menu (Start, Programs, Accessories, Systems Tools, Compression Agent).

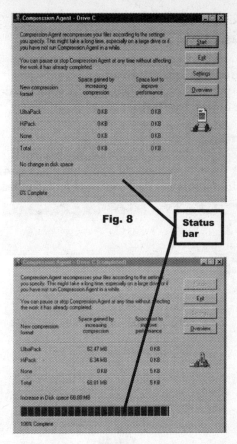

Fig. 8

Status bar

Fig. 9

Section 10:
System Tools: ScanDisk

Essential Information
The purpose of ScanDisk is to check your 3½" floppy disk or your hard disk for errors or damage.

Action 1
To open ScanDisk, go to **Start** on your taskbar and click once, then highlight **Programs**, **Accessories**, **System Tools** and then click once on **ScanDisk**.

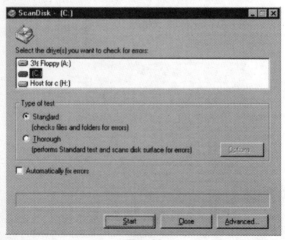

Fig. 10

Action 2

On the ScanDisk window (Fig. 10) there are two radio buttons for the type of test to be completed. The first, **Standard Test**, checks all files for errors and the second, **Thorough Test** performs the Standard Test and also scans your disk surface for errors.

Click once to place a tick in the check box 'Automatically fix errors'.

Action 3

Click once on **Start**. The computer will tell you when it has finished. If you do not want to run this program at the moment, click on the cross at the top of the window.

JARGON BUSTER

Backup
An extra copy of your data and programs.

BIOS
Basic Input/Output System. Permanently stored on the ROM chips inside the computer. Allows the computer to start.

Bit
Binary Digit. The smallest piece of information a computer can handle.

Byte
8 bits or approximately 1 character (i.e., a letter, space or number).

CD-ROM
Compact Disc Read Only Memory. A device storing a large quantity of information that can be read by any computer. Cannot be used for saving.

CD-R
Recordable CD. Can be used to store up to 650 MB of data.

CD-RW
A CD drive or player that will also write data onto recordable CDs.

Central processing unit
See CPU.

Characters per second (cps)
The speed of printers is measured in characters per second.

Chat rooms
'Virtual' meeting places for people who share views and interests.

Cheats
Shortcuts to becoming more proficient or winning at computer games.

Chip
A tiny piece of silicon with an electronic circuit engraved on it that can do different jobs within an electronic system.

Cookies
Small text files that are generated when you visit a web site. Contains very basic information about your visit.

CPU
Central Processing Unit. The main computer chip or 'brain' within the computer.

Cybercafé
Cafés that also have computers linked to the Internet, available for public use for a small charge.

Database

A type of program that organises sets of information.

Default

A preselected setting that the computer will open as its first choice.

Defrag/ Defragmentation

A process whereby a program within the computer rearranges the fragments of files which are stored in numerous places on the hard disk. The pieces of each file are stored next to each other.

Disk compression

A program that reduces the space that data takes up on the hard disk or floppy disk.

DOS

Disk Operating System. The most common operating system for IBM and compatible systems.

Dot pitch

Measurement of how close dots are placed on the monitor. The closer the dots, the better the image on the screen. Dot pitch is measured in millimetres.

Dots per inch (dpi)

Measurement of the quality of a monitor or printer. The higher the number of dots per inch, the better the quality.

Download

The action of copying files from the Internet onto your computer.

DVD

Digital Versatile Disk or Digital Video Disk. Can be used for multimedia and data storage.

Electronic mail (e-mail)

Messages sent from one computer to another over a network.

Emoticons

Small pictures used in e-mails to convey emotions.

Expansion slot

A slot at the rear of the computer that allows you to add and connect electronic expansion cards or boards to provide additional features to the computer.

FAQ

Frequently Asked Questions. Comes up on many programs to help you get started.

Floppy disk

A 3½" floppy disk is capable of storing 1.3 MB (megabytes of information).

Floppy drive

A slot in the front of the systems unit that takes a 3½" floppy disk enabling data to be retrieved or saved.

Font

The kind of typefaces available for text.

Font size

Different sizes of the same font.

Formatting toolbar

Enables text to be changed and moved.

Freebies or freeware

Free software available to download from the Internet.

FTP

File Transfer Protocol. A process that allows you to download and upload information as files to and from the Internet.

Game port

A connection at the back of the computer for a joystick, game pad, etc.

Gb-RAM

The amount of Random Access Memory measured in gigabytes.

Gigabyte (Gb)

1 billion bytes.

Gigahertz (Ghz)

The speed of your processor.

Hard drive or hard disk

The permanent storage device on your PC that holds programs and files.

Hardware

The physical components of the computer (monitor, mouse, systems unit, etc).

Hertz (Hz)

Cycles per second, used to measure frequency for monitors.

HTML

Hypertext Mark-up Language. The programming language used to create web pages.

IAP

Internet Access Provider.

I-beam

The shape of the pointer when it turns into a text cursor, ready for you to type.

Icon

A picture on the desktop that is the gateway to the program it represents.

Inkjet printer

A printer that sprays ink through tiny jets to create letters and characters.

Internet Café

Cafés that have computers linked to the Internet and are available for public use for a small charge.

IRC

Internet Relay Chat. A program that allows you to 'chat' in real time (as soon as you submit your message) on the Internet.

Joystick

A joystick plugs into the game port at the back of the computer and is used to control games programs.

Keyboard

A piece of computer hardware that allows communication between user and the computer.

Kilobyte (K or KB)

1,024 bytes, usually rounded down to 1,000 bytes.

Laptop

A portable computer smaller than a briefcase.

Laser printer

A printer that creates an image in the same manner as a photocopying machine.

Local area network (LAN)

Two or more computers connected together via cables. The connected computers can share information, printers, etc.

MB RAM

The amount of Random Access Memory measured in megabytes.

Megabyte

One million bytes. A byte is roughly 8 bits or one typed character. Memory is measured in megabytes (M or MB).

Megahertz (MHz)

The speed of the microprocessor is measured in megahertz.

Microprocessor

The main chip of the computer.

Millisecond (ms)

One thousandth of a second.

Modem

Stands for *mo*dulator and *dem*odulator. The modem changes a signal inside your computer to allow it to send and receive data over the telephone system.

Monitor

The TV-like screen that allows you to see your work. The size of the monitor is measured diagonally.

Motherboard

The main printed circuit board that covers the base of the systems unit, enabling all the electronic components to connect with each other.

Mouse
A device that controls the cursor arrow on the screen.

Multimedia PC
A PC that is ready to be connected to the Internet.
Would include CD-ROM drive, speakers and sound
card enabling the computer to play video, graphics
and sounds.

Nanosecond (ns)
One billionth of a second.

Newbie
A person who is new to the Internet.

Operating system
The program that operates behind the scene telling
the computer where to find files, etc. The most
common operating system for IBM compatibles is
DOS.

Palmtop
A hand-held computer.

Parallel port
A connection at the back of the computer most
commonly used to connect a printer.

Peripheral units or devices
Equipment that you connect to your computer, e.g.,
game pad, printer, scanner.

Port

Connection at the back of the systems unit used to plug in external devices like the mouse or scanner. There are two types: serial and parallel.

Processor

The main chip of the computer.

Protocol

The rules and regulations that govern communications with the Internet.

QWERTY

The standard letter keys found on typewriters and computers, named after the first six letters on the top line.

RAM

Random Access Memory. Temporary storage space where data can be deleted or overwritten.

ROM

Read Only Memory. Information that is permanently stored on chips within the computer and cannot be overwritten.

Scanner

The computer is able to copy an image placed onto the scanner. The image can then be viewed or used on documents.

Search engines

Enormous directories built automatically by a computer program, which combs the Internet for information.

Serial port

A connection at the back of the computer usually connected to the mouse or external modem that transmits data.

Shareware

Software to download to use for a limited period for free. If you like it, you can register your copy and pay a fee.

Smilies

Another word for emoticons.

Snail mail

The traditional postal service so-called because it is slower than e-mail.

Software

The programs within the computer.

Sound card

A printed circuit board that handles and produces sounds. Plugs into expansion slots inside the systems unit.

Spreadsheet

A program that handles number manipulation. Used, for example, for accounts budgets and cheque book balancing.

Systems unit

The box that holds all the electronic parts to make the computer work.

Virus

An unwanted piece of code attached to a program. Can infect and corrupt programs within the computer.

Web directories

Organised logical lists based on a variety of chosen categories. Each category is subdivided into further groups, which are again subdivided.

Wizards

Mini programs that give instructions and information about how to use more complex programs.

Word processing

The creation of documents, letters, files, memos, etc. using the computer.